BERLITZ®

KU-821-355

SINGAPORE

1990/1991 Edition

By the staff of Berlitz Guides

A Macmillan Company

How to use our guide

- All the practical information, hints and tips that you will need before and during the trip start on page 104.
- For general background, see the sections Singapore and the Singaporeans, p. 6, and A Brief History, p. 14.
- All the sights to see are listed between pages 24 and 50, with suggestions for day trips and longer excursions from Singapore from page 51 to 73. Our own choice of sights most highly recommended is pinpointed by the Berlitz traveller symbol.
- Entertainment, nightlife and all other leisure activities are described between pages 74 and 91, while information on restaurants and cuisine is to be found on pages 93 to 103.
- Finally, there is an index at the back of the book, pp. 126–128.

Text: Don Larrimore
Photography: Walter Imber; cover and p. 11 Singapore Tourist Promotion Board
Layout: Ernest Meyer
We wish to thank the Singapore Tourist Promotion Board for their help in the preparation of this guide. We're also grateful to Phan Lie-Tjhen and to the Permanent Mission of Singapore to the United Nations, Geneva, for their valuable assistance.
Cartography: Falk-Verlag, Hamburg.

Contents

Singapore and the Singaporeans

Sampans and skyscrapers. The fascinating contrasts are everywhere in this dynamic island Republic where East merges with West. Multiracial and multilingual, Singapore is one of the post-war world's great success stories.

But hurry. Every year there's less of the traditional oriental charm that enchanted Rudyard Kipling, Somerset Maugham and generations of other visitors. Although Singapore is a mere 136 kilometres above the equator, scant traces of tropical languor linger. Efficiency, discipline and order are the hallmarks of one of South-East Asia's cleanest and wealthiest countries.

Here you'll find an appealing mix of peoples and cuisines. Sights are exotic but not venerable, since today's Singapore was not founded until 1819. The shopping is superb for goods from around the globe, mostly duty-free. And when you're ready for a change of pace, Singapore is the ideal jumping-off spot for South-East Asia's most attractive resorts, Penang and Bali.

Lying just south of peninsular Malaysia, the Republic of Singapore comprises a main island and 54 islets. Across the Strait of Malacca, Asia's busiest shipping route, some islands of the Indonesian archipelago are visible on the horizon. Singapore covers a total area of 620 square kilometres, just

about the size of Chicago or the Isle of Man. Strategically located between the Indian Ocean and the South China Sea at the crossroads of east-west commerce, the Republic boasts one of the world's busiest ports and largest oil-refining centres. Thanks to a stable business-minded government, banking and industry are flourishing.

Orchids, the national flower, thrive in the humid heat. You may wilt. Most visitors are glad of the air-conditioning at ho-

Ferocity is all in fun at Chingay Parade, peak of Chinese New Year.

tels, restaurants and shopping centres, something the vast majority of Singaporeans live without. Temperatures stay high year-round, days averaging 30.6°C and nights 23.5°C. However, sea breezes moderate the steamy climate, as well as two annual monsoon rain periods.

Singapore island was once marsh and jungle. The north is still lush with equatorial foliage, while the centre has peaceful reservoirs and an extensive nature reserve, complete with reticulated pythons and king cobras. You won't see wild tigers (the last one was sighted in 1932), but you can still hear the crickets. Somehow they sound oriental.

A causeway spanning the Johore Strait links the island with Malaysia, one kilometre away. Across it by road, rail and pipeline comes most of the food and water supply for the Republic. The 20th century is gaining ground everywhere as land is

reclaimed from the swamp, sea and jungle for the construction of carefully planned industrial estates.

Teeming with most of the island's population, the city of Singapore is the headquarters for banks, airlines, travel agencies and businesses. Many are housed in modern towers along central Shenton Way. A garden city, Singapore has carefully programmed parks, green patches and rows of trees among the high-rise, low-cost housing estates that are home to about 80 per cent of the Republic's inhabitants.

All this makes for an unlikely skyline at the southern tip of mainland Asia, unimaginable during the century and a half of British colonial rule. Only a few institutions remain to fuel

Amidst all the sweeping modernism pedal-power and hand-kneading are still common Singapore sights.

nostalgia for that leisurely era, notably the cricket club fronting on the green expanse of the Padang, Victoria Theatre, Saint Andrew's Cathedral, the Supreme Court building and Raffles Hotel. Orchard Road, the cosmopolitan thoroughfare of today's hotel and tourist shopping district, retains none of the nutmeg and pepper plantations of the colonial past.

Modern Singapore is a tribute to its remarkable, preponderantly Chinese population. Three of every four of the Republic's 2.6 million citizens are descendants of immigrants from mainland China. Acumen and acupuncture only hint at their contribution. Another 15 per cent are Malays, while Indians make up about 6 per cent of the total. This is an energetic society, and a young one. A good many of the people weren't even born when Singapore became an independent republic in 1965.

Although Malay is the "national language", English as the language of administration and business is more widely used, certainly by Singaporeans who deal with tourists. Mandarin Chinese and Tamil are the other official languages. In addition six distinct dialects are spoken within the Chinese

community. Ethnic Indians speak five others.

Religion is omnipresent. There are more than 500 Chinese temples and dozens of other well-attended places of worship. The major faiths are Buddhism, Taoism, Islam, Hinduism and Christianity. In this amazing mosaic, tensions are minimal. By current world standards, Singapore is a model of racial and cultural harmony.

Except when pelting monsoons defeat umbrellas and

Landmark of Muslim Singapore: gilded domes and slender minaret of Sultan Mosque.

drainage canals, life is continually spilling into the streets.

A post-war baby boom brought population density in Singapore City and along the southern coast close to the highest in the world. For many years the government conducted a most effective family planning campaign, including legal abortion and severe economic penalties to parents who had more than two children. However, owing to a changing ethnic balance between the different communities and labour shortages, families are now encouraged to have two or more children "if they can afford it".

Visitors to the island are invariably warmed by the helpful friendliness of the Singa- **11** poreans, not to mention the smiles seen on attractive faces of every hue. You'll notice some initial social shyness, particularly among the Chinese. You'll also encounter some rather brusque manners, which aren't meant to be impolite, just quick and businesslike. A government-run courtesy campaign aims to polish up the "thank you" quotient, hitherto underdeveloped.

As elsewhere in Asia, there's a tendency to tell you what it's thought you want to hear, regardless of reality. This is considered polite. It can also cause perplexing East-West misunderstandings. Grains of salt should be taken liberally when talking to local people.

Singapore's children are far and away the Republic's most beautiful resource. Westerners marvel at the well-behaved children here. A crying child is a real rarity. Take a bus ride just after school hours with the inevitable swarms of uniformed youngsters carrying satchels. You won't believe there's no one supervising them. In restaurants even very

small children sit long and late without a trace of fuss at family dinners. However children may be brought up (testimony differs), it's clear that families are close and help each other.

People here are superstitious, particularly the older generations. Fortune-tellers are consulted as a matter of course about "auspicious" days for weddings and other major undertakings. In traditionalist homes floors go unswept on the first and second days of the

At every street corner you'll be reminded that Singapore today is the supreme melting pot of Asia.

12

Chinese New Year so good luck won't be whisked away.

You'll find a widespread preoccupation with money in Singapore—how much something costs, how large someone's salary is. The virtues of industriousness and achievement are preached to people here from an early age. But they find escapes from commercialism and the performance pressure-cooker: holiday festivals, funerals, parades, spirit mediums, food stalls and gadget hawkers all attract hordes of Singaporeans. You'll see them wearing everything from *cheongsams* to jeans and saris to safari suits, a colourful and changing society. From dawn to dusk, this small but vital Republic vibrates to a kaleidoscope of different sights and activities—no visitor can fail to be caught up by the infectious buoyancy and dynamism of this charming, hospitable people at the crossroads between East and West.

A Brief History

A legend in concrete: the Merlion at river mouth where it all began.

With its fine harbour and enviable geographic position, it was inevitable that Singapore would become a major Asian centre. But it took an uncommonly long time.

For many prehistoric centuries, Singapore was evidently just a stopping point on the north-south route taken by mainlanders migrating out along the island chain into the South Pacific. Neolithic peoples didn't make much of the island when they were here between 2,500 and 1,500 B.C., judging from the scarcity of archaeological finds.

About A.D. 200 a Chinese diplomat reported that Singapore was inhabited by cannibals with short tails. European accounts also mention the island, minus man-eaters. Some time after the 7th century, Buddhists of the Sri Vijaya empire in nearby Sumatra were the first to colonize the swampy island, calling it Temasek (Sea Town). When Chinese junks began carrying porcelain and pottery to South-East Asia in the 10th century, in exchange for aromatic products and spices, Temasek became a well-known trading station.

Legend has it that the Buddhist prince Nila Utama landed here a century later, thought he saw a lion on the shore and called the place *Singa Pura* (Malay-Sanskrit for Lion City). Alternatively it is claimed that Indian settlers wished to honour the sacred lion of the Hindu goddess Mariamman. Either way the name stuck, even though Singapore never had any wild lions. The good prince, they say, must have seen a tiger*.

The little port flourished until the 1360s when invaders from Java savagely sacked the settlement. Singapore reverted to jungle obscurity. For more than 400 years only pirates and fisherfolk had any use for it.

Enter Empire

Early last century Britain's growing South-East Asian empire needed a base which could challenge Holland's oriental trade monopoly. On January 28, 1819, Stamford Raffles, a senior colonial agent of the British East India Company,

* Today the emblem of the Singapore Tourist Promotion Board (STPB) is the Merlion, a lion with a fish tail, symbolizing how Sea Town became Lion City.

14

Raffles

Historian, cartographer, zoologist, botanist, linguist and British colonialist, Sir Thomas Stamford Raffles remains above all Singapore's father figure some 160 years after he founded the island's first European settlement.

Raffles was knighted for a definitive *History of Java*, which he wrote while Lieutenant Governor of that colony for five years until 1816. His memory is kept alive in Singapore by a profusion of busts, statues and paintings. A hotel, a lighthouse and a central square bear his name.

Raffles spoke, read and wrote Malay, which he learned on a voyage from England to Penang. He also immersed himself in local culture and customs and was an advocate of colonial responsibility.

Tragically, he lost his first wife and four children to disease in South-East Asia. En route home in 1824, his ship caught fire and 122 cases of research materials and specimens he had collected over the years were destroyed. He died in England in 1826 at the age of 44, shortly after helping to establish the London Zoo.

Plaque on this riverside marble likeness lauds Raffles' vision.

sailed into the mouth of Singapore River. He liked what he saw—a good natural anchorage just as handy to the Strait of Malacca as anything the Dutch had and a verdant island with only 150 Malay and Chinese fishermen-villagers. Raffles spoke fluent Malay, and in one week obtained permission to found a trading post by agreeing to pay rents to the *Temenggong*, or local governor, and the Sultan of Johore.

From the beginning Raffles was convinced that under British imperial rule a great destiny lay ahead for the tiny settlement. He helped matters along greatly by decreeing that "the port of Singapore is a free port and trade thereof is open to ships and vessels of every nation free of duty equally and alike to all".

Before summer, Indians and Chinese had set up the first bazaar of shops and *godowns* (warehouses). Raffles banned slavery, drew up a legal code and laid out plans for a central British government area with separate villages nearby for the Chinese, Hindus, Arabs and Bugis from the Celebes. Evidences of this original town-planning scheme remain today.

In four years the population leaped to nearly 10,000 and the port handled some 3,000 vessels. All of Singapore island was ceded to the British in perpetuity by an Anglo-Dutch spheres-of-influence treaty signed in August, 1824, six months after Raffles returned home to England.

Despite raging piracy, trade grew and with it Singapore's importance. In 1832 the island was made capital of the newly incorporated Straits Settlements, embracing Penang and Malacca and ruled by British India. But Singapore was hardly a haven of tranquillity. Violence among town-dwellers was frequent, and tigers prowled the countryside.

The first man to be killed by a tiger died in 1831. It was a sensation. By the 1850s when ever more pepper, fruit and nutmeg plantations were being hacked out of the jungles, tigers were killing 300 people a year. Many of the marauding beasts swam across the Johore Strait from the densely overgrown mainland.

Tea, Opium and Terror

Trade in opium provided the British East India Company with revenue for the purchase of Chinese tea, demanded in ever-greater amounts by thirsty customers in England. Opium, grown in India and shipped via Singapore, was also bartered **17** for tea. This controversial commerce exploded in the 1840–42 Opium War. After the defeat of China by Britain, the mainland was opened to opium traffic and Hong Kong took over from Singapore as a major processing centre.

Opium, whisky and gambling were the favourite vices of Singapore's chiefly Chinese population. The British administrators did little to discourage these pastimes, since they produced a rich harvest of taxes. Chinese "tax farmers" were given the job of collecting revenues. This led to the formation of secret societies, which began terrorizing the island, running rackets, extorting money from shop owners and warring among themselves, if not with other communities.

In Singapore's first major riot in 1851, some 500 people died as Chinese and Europeans fought each other. Three years later the death toll was 600 in even worse fratricidal Chinese violence. Often the troubles involved control over prostitution, which prospered in a population imbalanced by predominantly male emigration from China. The British didn't or couldn't stem much of the violence, nor the piracy which constantly plagued nearby waters.

Transfer

Meanwhile, Singapore's wealthy merchants began agitating against the East India Company. They feared the colonial overlords of India would impose shipping duties and thus eliminate Raffles' free port concept, so profitable for them. After a long campaign of petitions and delegations to London, the merchants succeeded in having Singapore and Malaya transferred from the authority of India. On April 1, 1867, Parliament formally made the Straits Settlements a Crown Colony directly controlled by London. And so it remained for about 80 years. The chief executive was a governor, assisted by British councillors and an indigenous civil service.

The opening of the Suez Canal in 1869 gave Singapore a tremendous economic boost. To handle the faster flow of East-West trade, the waterfront area was expanded and more workers were recruited from China. British officialdom was forever worrying about opium dens, gambling and brothels, but didn't appoint an English-Chinese interpreter until 1871. Walter Pickering was named to that position and became the first Protector of the Chinese six years later. For a decade, despite assassination attempts, he succeeded as no one before in enlisting the Chinese and their secret societies as responsible partners in island affairs.

Late in the century, Singapore's prosperity and population soared again as the rubber and tin industries were developed on the Malay peninsula. These commodities were distributed world-wide from Singapore by Chinese traders recently arrived from the mainland. There were still about 15 Chinese men for every woman, but the ratio steadily improved as more families immigrated to settle.

In 1895 the formation of the Federated Malay States effectively separated Singapore from Malaya. Some scholars feel that this caused many of the racial and political problems which have divided the two countries ever since.

The Early 20th Century
A good number of Singapore's "overseas Chinese" supported Sun Yat Sen when he advocated the overthrow of the Manchu dynasty in 1900. After Sun's successful revolution in 1911, some left-wing Chinese came to Singapore, fore-runners of the communists who were to play a key role in later internal political struggles.

But for Britain the major concern was international and naval. Locked in combat with Germany during World War I, London withdrew her capital ships from Asian waters, leaving Japan all but unchallenged by 1916. Although Britain decided in 1923 to build a naval base at Singapore, construction lagged until Japan demonstrated her increasing military strength in the invasion of Manchuria in 1931. The base wasn't operational until just before World War II and there was no powerful fleet in the area.

World War II
Late in 1941 Britain sent two warships, the battle-cruiser *Repulse* and the battleship *Prince of Wales*, to Singapore waters as a belated show of force and morale-booster. Several hours before Pearl Harbour, Japanese planes bombed a brightly illuminated Singapore, while Japanese forces attacked Hong Kong and landed in northeastern Malaya and southern Thailand. On December 10, the *Repulse* and the *Prince of Wales*, cruising without adequate air cover, were sunk by Japanese war planes off the Malayan coast. British troops were forced into a harrowing retreat down the Malay peninsula towards Singapore, pre- **19**

sumed by many to be Britain's invincible Far Eastern island fortress.

In fact, there were no defences along Singapore's northern shore facing the Johore Strait, which narrows in one area to less than 700 metres. Churchill later confessed that "the possibility of Singapore having no landward defences no more entered my mind than that of a battleship being launched without a bottom". He was "staggered" at the truth. This incredible situation resulted from General Arthur E. Percival's refusal to build fortifications. Commander of British forces in Malaya and perhaps the most unpopular Briton in Singapore's history, he thought their construction would be "bad for the morale of troops and civilians".

By January 31, 1942 Malaya was lost and the last of the British army, some 30,000 exhausted troops, filed over the 19-year-old causeway to Singapore. After eight days of air raids and frantic, last-minute British and Commonwealth efforts to dig in effectively, the Japanese invaded the island. On February 15, Percival surrendered to General Tomoyuki Yamashita. Singapore, renamed Syonan and incorporated in the Greater East

Asia Co-Prosperity Sphere, plunged into $3\frac{1}{2}$ years of cruelly severe occupation. The fall of Singapore climaxed what has been termed Britain's worst defeat of two world wars: the loss of some 138,000 troops, mainly as prisoners of war, in the ten-week Malayan campaign.

Singapore's only link with the mainland is this busy causeway.

On September 5, 1945, shortly after Japan's surrender to General MacArthur in Yokohama harbour, British and Indian troops landed on Singapore to a wildly cheering reception. About 32,000 prisoners of war and 4,500 civilian internees were released. Japanese General **21**

Susheiro Itagaki formally surrendered the region to Lord Louis Mountbatten, Supreme Allied Commander for South-East Asia, at the town hall a week later. (The ceremony is recreated in a waxwork exhibition on Sentosa Island.)

Post-war Problems, Independence, Prosperity

By war's end the writing was on the wall for the British empire. Singapore became a Crown Colony separate from Malaya in 1946, splitting up the former Straits Settlements. In 1948 the first elections were held on the island, for nine of the 22 seats on the Legislative Council. The remainder of the seats were filled by nomination and ultimate authority still rested with the British governor. Singapore-born residents now outnumbered immigrants for the first time in history and post-war babies quickly pushed the population past the million mark.

Moving towards democracy, Singapore escaped the worst of the protracted communist rebellion known as the Emergency, which bled the Malay peninsula from 1948 to 1960. In the 1955 elections, David Marshall, a lawyer, became Singapore's first Chief Minister when his Labour Front formed a coalition with the Malay Union Alliance to secure a majority of one in the new Legislative Assembly.

Once home rule was gained in 1959, the People's Action Party of Lee Kuan Yew was overwhelmingly victorious in elections, as it has been ever since. As Prime Minister, Lee in 1963 and 1965 guided the island into and out of union with newly formed Malaysia, during a period of bitter political turmoil which saw serious race riots.

On August 9, 1965 Singapore became a fully independent nation, joining the United Nations and the British Commonwealth soon after. The constitution was amended to make Singapore a republic in December of that year.

Since then there has been a headlong rush to modernize. Campaigns to clear city streets of litter, plant trees and discourage long hair worn by young men have changed the look of the new nation. Singapore's financial, maritime, communications and distribution services are in demand the world over. And the number of tourists arriving each year exceeds the 2.6 million population. Even Raffles might have been surprised at it all.

Sentosa's Surrender Chamber: the end of World War II in South-East Asia at Singapore Town Hall. **23**

What to See

Scattered about this little country are enough sights to occupy the average visitor for the better part of a week. Respecting the equatorial climate, you won't want to dash about. While agencies conduct daily guided tours from hotels to various attractions by bus, private car and taxi (all air-conditioned), you'll appreciate the full, fascinating flavour of Singapore only on foot, by boat and public bus (breeze-cooled through open windows). For short excursions only, you might try haggling down the price of a ride in one of the island's trishaws (bicycles with sidecars).

For a private tour, be sure your guide is one of the several hundred who wear a special badge and carry proof that they are trained and licensed by the STPB. All these authorized guides speak English.

Singapore City

To find your city bearings take a ride on public double-decker bus No. 141, which wanders from the Toa Payoh housing estate through the tourist hotel district and waterfront to the financial district and back. In fact, public buses go almost everywhere on the island. Frequent and inexpensive, they operate between dawn and midnight and are great fun except in rush hour.

Chinatown

Chinatown's 2½ square kilometres of cluttered streets are centred on South Bridge Road. Known locally as "Big Town" *(Tua Poh),* this is the heart of Singapore. Forget wheeled transport, take your camera and go both morning and evening when the markets, indoors and out, are liveliest. You'll happen upon hawkers selling live eels, gnarled ginger, *batiks,* decorated lanterns and freshly slaughtered python meat. There's a herbalist for whatever ails you. An old trishaw driver can tell you where to go.

Chinatown's prime religious attraction is **Sri Mariamman,** the oldest Hindu temple on the island. This much-photographed landmark on South Bridge Road, with its wooden tower, dates back nearly 150 years. It is dedicated to a goddess able to cure smallpox and cholera, former local scourges. During certain annual festivities you'll see impressive

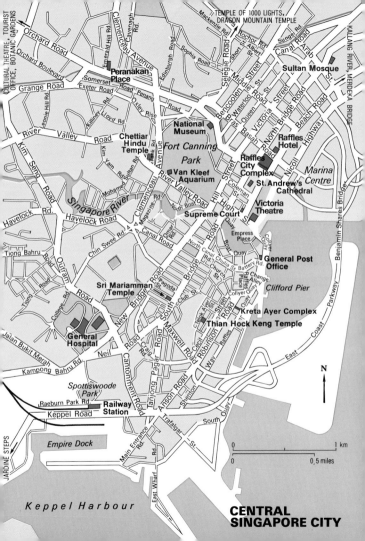

CENTRAL
SINGAPORE CITY

Sri Mariamman's sculpted tower is consummately Indian, the sausages of a recipe most decidedly Chinese.

Remedies and Superstitions

Chinatown's medicine shops provide the ultimate in oriental inscrutability. An outsider can only wonder at the potions made from dried reptiles, flowers, roots, barks and minerals. Medical wisdom accumulated for several thousand years dictates natural remedies prescribed and applied with serene confidence and utter disregard of modern science.

Some are effective. *Tchang cho yow* (green grass oil) massaged onto a sprained ankle or muscle affords rapid relief. However, countless Singaporeans affirm that the flesh of flying fox boiled in soup cures, or greatly relieves, asthma. Complexions and backache are thought to benefit from a diet of turtle soup. And to speed recovery from mumps, the Chinese character for "tiger" may be brushed onto the patient's cheek in black ink by someone born in the year of the tiger.

Many Chinese eat eel or celery steamed with herbs in a clay pot to reduce high blood pressure. Bird's nest, believed to provide vitality and cleanse the blood, is recommended for healthy lungs and during pregnancy. A costly powder of finely ground pearls is taken by girls between the ages of eight and 15 seeking a lustrous, pearly complexion.

Some Chinese medical men will tell you that such "cool" fruits as pineapples, melons, papayas and pears induce abortion in the first half of pregnancy. Aubergines (eggplant) are forbidden to people with bad eyesight and shellfish to anyone with a wound. Excessive amounts of tea or coconut water are also proscribed, lest knees weaken in old age.

Ginseng has been a major article of faith since Chinese emperors started taking it for longevity and sexual potency centuries ago. Western medical testing has not confirmed the twisted root's reputed curative powers, although it does help digestive problems. Ginseng is overwhelmingly popular and very expensive, and you'll see ginseng tablets, powders, extracts and tea on sale everywhere.

fire-walking here. This Hindu shrine adjoins the modest Chulia Mosque.

In **Sago Street** you'll find elaborate paper models of cars, mansions and other material riches, burned by the Chinese after funerals to accompany the deceased into the hereafter. **27**

Close by in **Sago Lane** ("Death House Alley") modern undertakers have replaced the death houses where some Chinese spent their dying days. They awaited death in the hired rooms where they were laid out and mourned by friends and relatives. Flaming funeral ceremonies are still performed after dark.

A dwindling number of shophouses are home and workplace for an ever-shrinking segment of the population. Decaying and unhygienic, these buildings are as old as the century. In their dim confines ancient Chinese crafts and customs are perpetuated.

As you stroll around, watch for the few surviving makers of papier-mâché masks and shiny wooden clogs, traditional Singapore footwear. In **Club Street,** craftsmen still carve gilt sandalwood statuettes of Buddhist and Taoist deities, which can cost thousands of Singapore dollars.

Colourful **Telok Ayer Street** features the oldest and most important Hokkien temple in Singapore, **Thian Hock Keng** (Temple of Heavenly Happi-

Traditional calligraphy remains a useful and respected profession. **29**

Whence Incense

In the old days, only emperors were considered close enough to the celestial gods to burn aromatic offerings to them. Today, lofty or lowly, the traditionalist Chinese light incense at temples, at home, even in modern offices. The devout do it daily, hoping for health, wealth and other blessings.

Incense comes in two forms: coils of processed sandalwood dust, which can burn for as long as a fortnight and joss sticks, which are thin bamboo sticks covered with wood dust. The odour varies and can be almost overpowering for the uninitiated.

As you'll realize in any Chinese temple, Singaporeans have a lot of wishes they think are worth lighting up for.

ness). The temple was built by immigrants from the Hokkien district of China, who carried the granite pillars and statue of the ocean-taming goddess Ma Chor Poh to Singapore from China in 1840. Here, as at every Chinese temple, you'll see the joss sticks and incense coils which worshippers burn as offerings. It's said that the smokier and more dust-laden the temple, the more popular and affluent it is. Singaporeans seeking divine blessings make donations; normally visitors do not.

For a small sum a Chinatown fortune-teller will decipher your palm or advise by horoscope on a marriage. A calligrapher will dash off a "lucky scroll" and an exorcist might drive away evil spirits with joss sticks and paper cutouts. There's even a spirit medium who goes into a trance most nights at a Taoist temple by the North Boat Quay, dispensing wisdom from the Monkey God who is said to possess him and cutting his own tongue with a sword, apparently without pain.

Until very recently this traditional way of life seemed in danger of disappearing completely from the Singapore scene. But a cry of protest went up when the old central market was demolished to make way for the high-rise **Kreta Ayer** shopping and residential complex (at the crossing of Smith and Trengganu streets). Now Chinatown is under order of preservation. And the market continues to thrive in its streamlined surroundings.

At Thian Hock Keng and all other temples, worshippers make offerings of food and joss sticks.

The Waterfront

The marvellous three-kilo-metre **Singapore River** travels through the heart of the city. Site of the island's earliest trading settlement and a former pirate haunt, the river is revered as the "soul of Singapore".

There's plenty going on—along the banks and on the river itself. Not so long ago the river was polluted and somewhat odoriferous, but in a clean-up campaign, *twakows* (bumboats) were banned from the river, and the antiquated buildings which lined it have been replaced by modern hotels and open-air cafés. Some bumboats have returned as tourist launches. River tours provide fascinating glimpses of the lower reaches of Singapore River.

The waterfront area in spite of all still has something of the atmosphere of the days when pirates and gunboats held sway. Take a stroll along the

river as it winds through the government and business districts down to the harbour.

No urban developer will disturb the white statue of Raffles in a small shaded park on the east bank behind Parliament House.

Guarding the busy river mouth is the statue of the half-fish, half-lion Merlion, the symbol of Singapore. At dusk when it's lighted, young couples like the benches in Merlion Park, on a little promontory. Beyond is Elizabeth Walk and Marina City. Harbour-watching is excellent any time along Collyer Quay or Benjamin Sheares Bridge.

Vessels from all over the world ornament Singapore's great **harbour.** Even confirmed landlubbers will want to take a close look at this nautical extravaganza: hundreds of ocean-

Junks, rare now, were not speedy and Singapore harbour was for swimming.

going vessels at anchor, a horizon-full of tonnage flying the flags of all the sailing nations.

To enjoy the show, take one of the daily harbour cruises by motorized junk, which lasts about 2½ hours, passing interesting wharves, a few southern islands and countless scows, freighters, water-taxis, police boats, tugs, schooners, yachts and super-tankers supplying the Republic's oil refineries. There are also 1-hour cruises of the harbour stopping at Sentosa Island. Boats leave from Clifford Pier.

Your junk may use its raucous horn to shoulder through traffic. An interesting vessel is the Chinese *tongkang,* which has an eye painted on it so that the boat can "see" where

You can haggle for anything in colourful, crowded Change Alley.

it is going. You used to see many more as they transported cargo to land from the ships anchored out in the Singapore Roads, but now giant cranes have made them virtually redundant. At some stage the engine will cut out and your junk will lumber pleasantly along.

Clifford Pier is endlessly busy and entertaining. It's sited at one end of **Change Alley,** a partly elevated shopping corridor where hard-sell and hard

bargaining prevail. A pickpocket's dream, Change Alley is narrowest as it disgorges into Raffles Place. This former city hub has been given some neoclassical structures marking the entrance to the downtown Mass Rapid Transit System station.

Fort Canning Park District

On Tank Road opposite Fort Canning Park is the **Chettiar Hindu Temple,** Singapore's richest, dedicated to the six-headed god, Lord Subramaniam. It's also one of the city's newest. The former mid-19th-century temple building has been demolished and a new edifice has gone up. Here you'll see a cobra of pure hammered gold entwined around a four-foot-high **peacock,** a stunning treasure. Traditionally, the Chettiar temple is the focal point of penitents' processions during the Thaipusam festival in January or February.

Chettiar is a South Indian term for money-lender. And this occupation is practised just down the way at No. 1 Tank Road, in an intriguing establishment where licensed money-lenders sit white-robed and shoeless on floor mats beneath ceiling fans.

The **Van Kleef Aquarium** (off River Valley Road, in Fort **35**

Canning Park) is a small marine collection of some 4,000 specimens. The sleepy star is a grey nurse shark, which shares space with large turtles fond of perching on its back. The sight of a pen of crocodiles will greet you, followed by a tank of Sudanese piranhas and electric eels. Swimming around with the sting-ray are "Painted Sweetlips" and "Clown Sweetlips". Winner of the name game is the tiny "Banded Nandid" near by. Oddest creature is the "Feathery Filefish", reddest the "Fantail Lionhead" from China and prettiest probably the yellow, black and silver "Poor Man's Moorish Idol".

You'll enjoy at least an hour at the century-old **National Museum** across the park from the Aquarium on Stamford Road. There is a fascinating display of the history, ethnology and art of Singapore and South-East Asia. Watch for aromatic products and Chinese trade porcelain from the Sung, Yuan and Ming dynasties (960–1644). You'll see magnificent tableware and rosewood and mother-of-pearl furniture

Singaporean children wear traditional uniforms and bright smiles.

from the Ch'ing dynasty (1644–1911). There are old Chinese beds, exotic stringed instruments, gongs and drums and the **jade collection** amassed by the Aw brothers, the Tiger Balm ointment millionaires. Two green jadeite discs of Hsi Wang Hu, Queen of the Western Heaven, and a hand-carved table screen of the same material are greatly admired by experts.

The remarkable "Silver Boat with 20 Men" from Brunei is found in an upstairs gallery. Air-conditioned wings house the National Art Gallery and Singapore University's collection of regional pottery, decorative textiles and religious statuary. Also on exhibit is the "Revere Bell", presented to Saint Andrew's Cathedral in Singapore by Paul Revere's daughter, who was the wife of the first U.S. consul on the island. Cast in 1843 at the Revere foundry in Boston, the bell sounded Singapore's curfew.

Photographers will appreciate the façade of the **Chinese Chamber of Commerce** nearby on Hill Street. Two stone lions guard this replica of Peking's Imperial Palace wall, which has two sets of nine purple, yellow and red dragons. (When you're taking pictures here and elsewhere around town, beware

Dragon robe (National Museum) brought wearer luck. Right: Bus stop in Arab Street.

of open monsoon drainage canals!)

Living witness to a bygone era, the **Raffles Hotel** of 1886 with its shaded courtyards and cool verandahs is a Singapore institution on Beach Road, haunted by the ghosts of Maugham, Kipling and Conrad. And the Singapore Sling!

Muslim Singapore

Within ten years of Singapore's founding, the area around Arab Street developed into a thriving Arab village known as Kampong Glam. You won't find unmixed descendants of Singapore's 19th-century Arab traders here, since most of them intermarried with Malays or Indian Muslims. But the shops crammed with baskets, *batik* and baubles will remind you of a Middle-Eastern bazaar.

The minarets and domes of the Sultan Mosque in North Bridge Road near Arab Street, dominate this mainly Muslim area. You'll want to explore the cool, carpeted interior of Singapore's largest mosque and check the time in Mecca on a modern clock. Fridays, the Muslim sabbath, are most interesting: robed worshippers flood in, responding to the resounding prayer call of the *muezzin*. Near the mosque herbalists offer potions you won't find in Chinatown and scent-sellers have everything from local leaves to Parisian perfume. Several Indian Muslim restaurants in the area specialize in *murtabah*—India's answer to the pizza.

Take time to wander nearby streets like Baghdad, Bussorah and Muscat—all a short distance from the mosque. This evocative section of Singapore preserves some fine houses, traditional Muslim businesses and religious schools.

Orchard Road District

Singapore's smart shopping and hotel district centres on Orchard Road, a wide, tree-shaded thoroughfare lined with soaring buildings. You'll probably want to spend most of your time browsing in the air-conditioned comfort of Orchard Road's high-rise shopping complexes. But don't miss out on the nostalgic

Orchard Road's high-rise shopping centres draw the crowds. So do the demonstrations at the Singapore Handicrafts Centre (right).

shopping possibilities at **Peranakam Place** (at the crossing of Emerald Hill). Several antique dealers have taken over this row of old Malaccan-style shops, declared a national monument. There's also an interesting little museum here, dedicated to the lifestyle of the Straits Chinese (descendants of Chinese immigrants and Malay women).

Orchard Road runs into Tanglin Road, where the **Singapore Handicraft Centre** sells all manner of handicrafted articles (see p. 78). Musicals, jazz and pop concerts top the bill at the Singapore Cultural Theatre, nearby in Grange Road.

The Malayan rubber industry got its start at the **Botanic Gardens** when 22 Brazilian seedlings were imported via Britain's Kew Gardens. You can see two ageing rubber trees which long ago surpassed the average life span of 30 years. You can also examine the orchid centre, where hybridization experiments began in 1928. In the gardens on Holland Road are ornamental plant pavilions, an outstanding palm collection, a cannonball tree, a sausage tree and swans on a lily-covered lake. This is Singapore's oldest public park, founded in 1859.

Points North

To imagine what Singapore was like before colonization, wander off on your own for a two-hour hike in **Bukit Timah Nature Reserve** (upper Bukit Timah Road, 12 km. from Singapore City), the last primeval forest left on the island (come

early to avoid the midday heat) and, at 163 metres, the highest point on Singapore Island.

Orchids grow outdoors year-round at the **Mandai Orchid Gardens** on Mandai Lake Road, in the rural northern area of Singapore. Boxes of the exotic blooms, most of which are regional hybrids, can be shipped from the privately owned gardens to Australia and European countries.

Families crowd the leafy **Zoological Gardens** at feeding time on Sundays and holidays. Enjoy shows featuring sea lions, chimpanzees, hippos, elephants and orangutans. Polar bears and tigers are favourite attractions among the 500 or so animals. Public buses 171 and 137 go north through palm-fringed countryside to the zoo.

Sembawang, one of Singapore's most pleasant areas, is a 30-minute drive north from the city centre. Here several unspoilt Malay villages, called *kampongs*, are scattered about green and serene countryside, far from urban noise and air pollution. You'll see brightly painted wooden houses on stilts surrounded by neat gardens of mangoes, durians, bananas and rambutans. Chickens, cats and a few monkeys roam freely. Palms are everywhere, a reminder that this used to be coconut as well as rubber country. Barefooted children grin "hello" and then go back to splashing in the sea. Although the district is mostly Malay, there are also Chinese and Indian merchants in Sembawang, along with foreign expatriates who have opted for rural residence in this northern corner of the island.

The West Coast

The **Tiger Balm Gardens** *(Haw Par Villa)* cover the hills of several seaside hectares, on Pasir Panjang Road. Brightly painted plaster figures illustrate complicated epics and tell you all you want to know about Chinese mythology. Moralizing slogans abound: "Debauchery: The shortest cut to Poverty and Degradation is through Wine and Women". Reminders to buy Tiger Balm are everywhere in this supernatureland. An ointment for muscular aches and pains, Tiger Balm made the fortune of the garden's donors, the brothers Aw Boon Haw (The Tiger) and Aw Boon Par (The Leopard). Group excursions don't give you enough time in this Chinese Disneyland but it's easy to reach by bus.

SINGAPORE ISLAND

At the **Ming Village** (32 Pandan Road) artisans make reproductions of famous porcelain, demonstrate the arts of calligraphy and perform the rituals of the tea ceremony. Before visiting, telephone 265 77 11 to arrange a conducted tour.

Walk among the rock gardens and quiet carp pools of the **Japanese Garden** *(Seiwaen)* on a 13-hectare island in Jurong Lake. The world's largest Japanese garden outside Japan, it has 36 harmonious features, each with a poetic Japanese name like "the peak where auspicious birds like to gather". The Japanese Garden adjoins the Chinese Garden.

At the **Chinese Garden** *(Yu Hwa Yuan)* you can climb six tiers to the top of the Cloud-Piercing Pagoda, which offers the best panorama of the lovely island garden. You'll see the Moon-Receiving Tower, the Fragrance-Filled Lily Pond, the Jade-Splashed Bridge, red and yellow pavilions and white stone boats. It all follows Sung dynasty (A.D. 960–1279) garden design and has something of the style of the Peking Summer Palace. Soft Chinese music

Exotic blooms and song birds can be admired at Mandai Orchid Garden and Jurong Bird Park.

All About Orchids

Although they grow wild throughout the world in thousands of varieties, orchids were first cultivated about 85 years ago, in Singapore. Hardier than most flowers, orchids take four to eight years to bloom. They may have no particular fragrance, although many tropical species have pungent, even offensive scents. Plants range from about one-half centimetre to six metres in height. Species are found near mountain snow and in tropical jungle.

Singapore, pioneer in orchid hybridization, has become Asia's main orchid exporting centre. Less perishable are the popular "Risis" orchids, which have been developed in the Republic. These are the selected flowers of some 500 varieties, electroplated in gold and fashioned into jewellery.

accompanies your stroll or stop at the Tea House. For Westerners this is a lulling, completely Chinese experience.

The **Jurong Bird Park** is said to be the finest of its kind in Asia. The highlight is an inflight netted aviary, at 2 hectares quite a considerable affair, where you can wander past a man-made waterfall among cockatoos and parakeets, bulbuls and water hens. **45**

Look for the gloriously coloured macaws and the penguins splashing about in their chilled-water enclosure. A tram with taped commentary trundles you around the landscaped park, planned by London Zoological Society specialists. It's included on some group tours and worth the long bus ride from town.

In its hundreds of displays, the **Singapore Science Centre** off Jurong Town Hall Road

Mushrooming in popularity, batik has spread from Indonesia, Malaysia and Singapore throughout the world, but the original is unsurpassed.

deals with everything from the mysteries of the universe to the wonders of aviation. Audio-visual aids, microcomputers and other gadgetry make a visit to the centre both interesting and informative.

If you're an early riser, the Jurong fish market not far away is best before 6 a.m.

The East Coast

Head away from the new high-rise buildings along the seaside "Golden Mile" towards sweeping **Benjamin Sheares Bridge,** part of the East Coast Parkway. You'll have a panoramic view of the city and the harbour. The east coast area has undergone massive reclamation, and beaches now line the coast almost up to Changi. Local people swim at the **East Coast Park,** just 20 minutes from central Singapore City. Some 300 hectares have been developed with excellent sports facilities.

On the way to CHANGI, organized East Coast tours take you either to a *batik* or a gem-cutting-and-polishing factory, where final products are on sale.

At Changi Airport, Singapore's exotic history is brought vividly to life in the **"Singapore Experience",** a dramatization on film of the island-nation's past. You'll be entertained by a parade of colourful personalities and you'll have a greater understanding of the events that have gone into the making of modern Singapore.

You need special authorization to visit the chapel of Changi Prison where both **47**

Styles differ but Buddhist faith is the same at venerable 1,000 Lights and Dragon Mountain Temples.

European civilians and military prisoners were interned in severe hardship by the Japanese during World War II. At the liberation, Mountbatten addressed the P.O.W.s from the Changi rooftop, which overlooks the notorious cellblocks.

Changi village, called "Little London" when British forces were stationed in the area, now has a modern shopping complex with good food stalls.

In Upper Serangoon Road you'll see Singapore's largest **crocodile farm.** About 400 of the beasts are displayed, along with some alligators, a pet python and an iguana. (Danger! Keep your hands out of the pools!) If given the chance, crocodiles could live for more than 100 years. Generally they're not and don't. When the crocodiles are between 3 and 7 years old,

they're killed and their skins are treated, dyed and polished before export or use in the bags and accessories you may inspect and buy here. Raised primarily for their skins, crocodiles can also be eaten. The meat tastes rather like chicken and is a delicacy to some.

Singapore's largest statue of Buddha, a 15-metre giant robed in yellow and adorned with countless electric lights, overwhelms you at the **Temple of 1,000 Lights** *(Sakya Muni Gaya)* further along on Race Course Road. You'll also see a mother-of-pearl replica of the enormous footprint Buddha left on Adam's Peak in Sri Lanka and a piece of bark said to have come from the sacred 2,500-year-old Bodhi tree. For a small donation you can spin a wheel of fortune or "light a long joss stick for a long life". Built in 1927 by a Siamese monk, the temple is now a blend of Chinese and Indian religion. Don't remove your footwear here, in **49**

In the aquarium or the frying pan, a fish will delight a Singaporean.

case your shoes walk away without you. Many public buses and East Coast coach tours go to this popular attraction.

Diagonally across Race Course Road (which has four temples but no horse track) is **Dragon Mountain Temple** *(Leong San Sze)*, one of the city's most exotic temples, with dramatic, colourful roofs. A plump and laughing gilt Buddha greets you and friendly Chinese-speaking attendants will point out the noteworthy wood carvings high in the main shrine. Try to go to the vegetarian feast on the tenth day of each Chinese calendar month. A monk chants scriptures every day at this delightful temple built with funds raised by merchants who emigrated from the Hokkien district of China.

Short Excursions

Offshore Islands

Ferries of various sizes link the city with satellite islands. For more obscure spots in the Strait of Singapore you may have to book with a boatman a day in advance. About half of the little islands are inhabited. Avoid week-ends when picnicking families flock to the islet beaches, as well as stormy weather.

While most of Singapore's remaining *kelongs* stand off the northern shore, you may pass one on a southern island cruise. Once there were hundreds of these primitive but efficient fishing traps with their rows of tall *nibong* palm stakes, *attap* huts and huge underwater nets. Watching the resident fishermen haul up the nets is best at night when the *kelong's* bright lights lure a big catch.

Sentosa is an elaborately developed resort island covered with tropical greenery just half a kilometre south of Singapore. The contrast with the metropolitan rat-race is striking on Sentosa, which means "tranquillity" in Malay.

Instead of the six-minute ferry, take the Swiss-built **cable car** from the waterfront station at Jardine Steps (the terminal at Mount Faber is less convenient, though you'll enjoy the view from the summit, particularly in the late afternoon and evening). A red-carpeted lift rises to the platform, where cheery attendants will help you into the swaying six-seat cabins. Soaring slowly some 60 metres above the busy ship channel and Keppel Harbour, you'll admire a panorama stretching from Sentosa out to distant Indonesian islands.

Formerly a British fortress built to protect the colonial harbour (the Japanese, however, came from the north), today Sentosa is dedicated to pleasure. A monorail links all the island's attractions. It takes just over half an hour to make the circuit. A commentary on the island is given in English and Mandarin. A seaside **Coralarium** in an air-conditioned pavilion built of coral houses more than 2,000 sea shells, including the rare Gloria Maris specimen.

Beyond the satellite tracking station is an 18-hole golf course close to holiday chalets. The interesting **Maritime Museum** has outstanding models of a 14th-century Arabian *sambuk*, an opium clipper and a Kiangsu junk. The **Surrender Chamber** is a must for history enthusiasts. There are displays **51** of 27 life-sized wax figures of the military men present at Japan's surrender and wartime mementoes. The **Pioneers of Singapore Museum** in the grounds presents the island republic's history, beginning with the 14th century.

On Sentosa you'll find South-East Asia's largest roller-skating rink, old Fort Siloso with underground tunnels and exotic weaponry, an art centre, an insectarium with butterfly farm, a nature trail, a protected swimming lagoon, golf courses, a musical fountain, a food centre, a campsite and beautiful sunsets.

Happily, Singapore's developers seem to have forgotten **Pulau Seking** (Seking Island). You won't. This idyllic gem is 40 adventurous and rather uncomfortable minutes by bumboat south of Jardine Steps. Seking drowses under tall palms. The islet's several hundred inhabitants, almost all Malay, live in wooden stilt houses breezily unencumbered by glass windows. A *sampan* is tied to each house. Cats, cockerels and goats wander freely, watched by songbirds and a few monkeys in homemade cages.

The few dozen televisions function only at night, as electricity is not available before 6 p.m. or after midnight. There

are no wheeled vehicles or public telephones. You may see the water supply arriving in drums by lighter from a neighbouring island. Or the nurse on her fortnightly visit. In the 20 minutes it takes to explore Seking, you'll see the *imam* and his small mosque, and the friendly *penghulu* (headman), who

Malay stilt houses encourage ventilation, discourage reptilean guests.

can't think of any reason why he and his villagers would want to live anywhere but in this tropical paradise.

Kusu, shaped like the tortoise it's named after, is a popular and unusual islet about 45 minutes by ferry south of Singapore. On Kusu's two hillocks, a Taoist temple of the prosperity god Tua Pek Kong and a Malay shrine or *kramat* are the stuff of legends. It seems an Arab and a Chinese were ship- **53**

Surprisingly, despite Singapore's insatiable and growing demand for shellfish, centuries-old netting techniques have scarcely changed.

wrecked on Kusu, where they lived in peaceful isolation until they died. They could have been holy men, but even if not their memories are honoured and the island is thought to harbour good spirits.

Kusu may have been where Raffles first landed. The two old houses of worship, dating back almost that far, attract masses of picnicking worshippers during the weeks before and after the annual Double Ninth Festival (9th day of the ninth moon, usually in October). But people go all year to the reclaimed sandy beach and the tortoise sanctuary.

Singaporeans flee the concrete and automobile fumes to **St. John's, Lazarus, Sisters** and **Hantu.** They go to these southern islets and some other reclaimed reef-isles for outdoor sports. St. John's, thus far the most developed, has holiday camps.

Pulau Ubin (Ubin Island), a short ferry trip from the village of Changi, is another place where rural village life is still very much intact.

Over the Causeway

Minutes north of Singapore you plunge into the markedly different atmosphere of peninsular Malaysia. How many minutes depends on how much traffic is crawling across the causeway to be processed by customs and immigration at the other end. (You can relieve tedium by watching—but not photographing—Singapore's narcotics-sniffing dogs at work on baggage.) If you're not hiring a car, coach tours from major hotels run regularly to southern Malaysia, as well as public bus No.170.

The half-day tours cover only JOHORE BAHRU, a jumble of a town immediately over the Strait. Here you'll see saucy advertisements and the periodicals not permitted in Singapore, litter-strewn streets, far more women wearing the colourful Malaysian *sarong kebaya* and fewer signs in English.

You will have to make advance arrangements to visit the Istana, the palace of the Sultan of Johore, richest of Malaysia's nine sultans and reputedly among the world's dozen or so wealthiest men. However, you may stroll any day in his palm gardens and admire his replica of a Japanese tea house. Now used only for ceremonies, the 110-year-old Istana contains a staggering collection of platinum, gold and silver tableware, not to mention the world's only crystal table and chairs. Local people state proudly that the Sultan owns several hundred polo ponies and a stable of motorcars, including the greatest vintage models. Wealth, enormously augmented by rubber plantations, has been in the family ever since Raffles paid the first rent to the ancestor of the current sultan.

At the small zoo nearby are several large Bengal tigers (very few of this officially protected species remain in Malaysia's jungle preserves), black bears and elephants. The hilltop **Abu Bakar Mosque,** where you'll be given covering for bare limbs, would resemble a ballroom were it not for the prayer rugs. The unusual columns and ceilings were constructed of eggshell mixed with plaster and cement. Visits to small *batik* and *songket* (brocade) factories **55**

Attire may be basic, but smiles are genuine in Malaysia's countryside.

are also included on Johore Bahru tours.

Less frequent full-day tours from Singapore go farther north to **Ulu Tiram Estate,** where you immerse yourself in the appealing life of rubber and palm oil plantations and enjoy a typical Malay luncheon. Seeing the densely planted countryside, you won't doubt that Malaysia is the world's largest rubber producer.

En route to or from Malaysia you might stop south of the causeway at the **Kranji War Memorial,** where some of the Allied servicemen killed in South-East Asia in World War II are buried on a long, sloping hillside beneath a stark monument. (All the dead are listed on the walls and in the registry of this cemetery, maintained by the Commonwealth War Graves Commission.)

clude transportation, hotel and sightseeing. There are also a few cruise ship opportunities from Singapore.

Malacca

The picturesque port of Malacca was once the largest town in South-East Asia and there is as much to see here as anywhere in Malaysia. You can walk in narrow, twisting streets that date back to its founding in the 15th century by a Sumatran prince. At that time traders speaking dozens of languages gathered in the bazaar to barter for precious stones, gold, silver and copper.

In 1511, Portuguese soldiers laid siege to the town, conquering it after a bloody ten-day battle. Their descendants continue to live in the "Portuguese Village", a few kilometres south-west of the city centre on the coast road. If you continue south on this road, you will have a good view of Mount Ophir, or Gunong Ledang, site of the first rubber plantation on the peninsula, begun with seedlings from Singapore.

The Portuguese built a fortress during their occupation, but all that remains is a gateway marking the site of the original harbour, now silted in. Saint Paul's Church, another reminder of Portuguese supre-

Long Excursions

Fanning out to destinations in South-East Asia is easy from Singapore. If the region's key centres aren't included on your air ticket, you'll find convenient and inexpensive flights from the Republic and, in the case of Malaysia, train, boat and bus service as well.

Local travel agents run a variety of package tours lasting anywhere from a week-end to a fortnight. These normally in-

macy, is also in ruins. Saint Francis Xavier is said to have preached here.

Most of Malacca's famous sights date from the period of Dutch domination, which began about 1640. The 17th-century **Stadthuys,** one of the oldest European buildings in Asia, still houses the chief government offices. You will find the symbol of Malacca—a Hindu relic called the Makara stone—in the Stadthuys grounds. Nearby is **Christ Church,** also built by the Dutch. As you walk through the streets of the town centre you'll come across gracious old houses with beautiful carved doors.

But it is nevertheless a Chinese flavour which prevails in Malacca. The first Chinese to arrive were envoys sent in 1409. They were followed by many of their countrymen, as you'll see at **Bukit China,** one of the largest and oldest graveyards outside the mainland. You'll find the most ancient Chinese temple in Malaysia in the heart of the town, the 18th-century **Cheng Hoon Teng.** Be sure to look up at the ceiling, decorated with porcelain and glass floral and animal motifs. There are many interesting shops and old Chinese clan houses in the surrounding district.

The **Tranquerah Mosque** close by, one of the oldest in Malaysia, attests to the strength of Islam in Malacca, where Muslim festivals are celebrated with particular zeal. The 19th-century Sultan of Johore, who sold Singapore to Raffles, is buried in the mosque.

The 600 years of Malaccan history are best appreciated through exhibits in the small **Museum,** housed in a historic building near the site of the original harbour. To ensure a return visit to this historic town, toss a coin in the **Sultan's Well,** dug in the 13th century, and you will come back to Malacca one day.

Penang

The green hills of Malaysia's premier holiday island are an abrupt contrast to low-lying Singapore, just an hour away by air. From a distance Penang with all its tropical vegetation barely seems inhabited. And by Singapore standards it isn't. About half a million Chinese, Malays and Indians live on this 285-square-kilometre island just off the north-western coast of Malaysia. Penang is called the "Pearl of the Orient" and some visitors fall in love with the island at first sight.

Less than 60 fishermen and

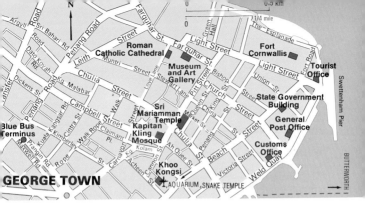

pirates were here in 1786 when Captain Francis Light founded Britain's first trading station on the Malay peninsula. He obtained eager native assistance in clearing ground for a settlement by firing silver coins from a cannon into the thick jungle. The outlines of the original wood stockade built by Light are marked by the stone walls of Fort Cornwallis, today a national monument.

George Town

Asia's longest bridge links Butterworth on the Malaysian mainland to George Town, Penang's capital, a crowded, increasingly high-rise yet essentially Chinese city. Most of the island's trishaws roam its raucous, bazaar-like streets. They're pleasingly inexpensive after Singapore, but by all means bargain with your driver before he pedals off. The best ways to travel around town are by trishaw and on foot.

You'll find the famed and fantastic **Khoo Kongsi** (Dragon Mountain Hall) in a courtyard off Cannon Street. This gilt Chinese clan house continues to provide people of the same surname with a centre for help and worship.

In contrast, the **Kapitan Kling Mosque** nearby on Pitt Street celebrates Indian-Moorish architecture, while the **Sri Mariamman Hindu Temple** on Queen Street features a huge, multi-hued pyramidal tower, in South Indian style. **59**

Rewards await visitors to Penang's small **Museum and Art Gallery** on Farquhar Street. Of particular interest are the splendid old mahjong set, the traditional Chinese bridal chamber in good-luck red and the ebony and mother-of-pearl furniture.

An enormous 33-metre-long **reclining Buddha** draws streams of visitors to the **Wat Chayamangkalaram** Siamese temple on Burmah Lane, a short distance from central George Town. Among the world's largest, the smiling Buddha is made of painted cement and has eyes and toe nails of pearl.

Forty prominent donation boxes surround the statue. A modest contribution puts your name plaque on the temple wall, though it's more expensive to have your ashes deposited in a cubicle inside the Buddha. Four dragons outside the main entrance guard this temple—and that's where photographers must stand to shoot the statue, unless the monks grant permission for interior photos.

Island Highlights

Seventy-four kilometres of good road meander around Penang. Guided tours make the circuit in about 4 hours, giving once-over-lightly treatment to a handful of sights. Exploring by hired car is better but costlier. Public buses are great value, but not always convenient. It takes four to five hours in riding time alone, not counting stops.

Once away from George Town you'll know you're on a Malay island. As you skirt the high central hills, you'll pass through rubber plantations, where the trees are tapped before dawn (except on rainy days when the latex would be washed away). Rice nurseries and paddy fields give way to groves of tapioca, nutmeg, cloves, bananas, pineapples and betel nuts. The atmosphere is equatorially rural.

Pride of Penang and among the largest Buddhist shrines in South-East Asia is **Kek Lok Si** (Temple of Paradise). Its serene hilltop location is impressive. Ignore if you can the souvenir shops along the upward slope to the temple precinct. Persevering up past sacred tortoise and fish ponds and many altars, you'll reach Maitreya, a laughing, bare-bellied golden Buddha with a supporting cast of four characters, also of gold. More Buddhas, *lohans* and other exotic figures line the way up to a sign on the uppermost terrace proclaiming the "Million Buddhas Precious Pa-

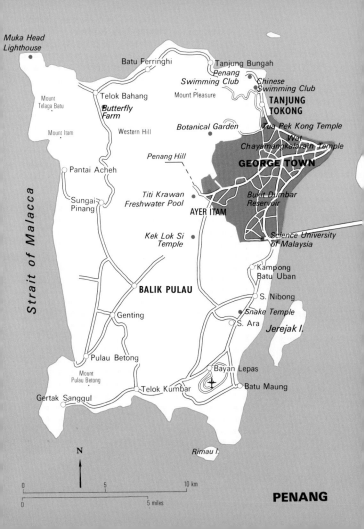

Muka Head
Lighthouse

Batu Ferringhi

Tanjung Bungah

Penang
Swimming Club

Chinese
Swimming Club

**TANJUNG
TOKONG**

Telok Bahang

*Butterfly
Farm*

Mount
Telaga Batu

Mount Pleasure

Mount Itam

Western Hill

Botanical Garden

Tua Pek Kong Temple

*Wat
Chayamangkalaram Temple*

GEORGE TOWN

Pantai Acheh

Penang Hill

Sungai
Pinang

*Titi Krawan
Freshwater Pool*

AYER ITAM

*Bukit Dumbar
Reservoir*

Strait of Malacca

*Kek Lok Si
Temple*

*Science University
of Malaysia*

BALIK PULAU

*Kampong
Batu Uban*

S. Nibong

Snake Temple

Genting

S. Ara

Jerejak I.

Pulau Betong

Mount
Pulau Betong

Bayan Lepas

Gertak Sanggul

Telok Kumbar

Batu Maung

Rimau I.

N

0   5   10 km

0   5 miles

PENANG

goda", dedicated to all Buddhas. To climb this Chinese-Thai-Burmese pagoda 30 metres high you should pay a monk a token sum. At the top you'll be rewarded with a beautiful view of the temple complex, forested hills, George Town and the sea beyond.

Take the No. 1 public bus from George Town to AYER ITAM village for a fraction of the taxi fare. You'll want to explore the market stalls and rural area at the foot of the temple hill.

The bottom station of the **Penang Hill Railway** is a short No. 8 bus ride from Ayer Itam. Even the Swiss won't be bored by the magnificent funicular to the 830-metre summit. The panorama takes in the island and rugged mainland scenery. Allow several hours to get away from it all.

Penang's **Snake Temple** is said to be unique. Listless pit vipers, tranquillized by incense, coil around altars and joss stick stands. The most deadly of

local species, these vipers feed on fresh eggs left for them in the sanctuary which they sometimes vacate at night. Visitors touch or handle the snakes at their own risk, but those who wish can be photographed holding defanged vipers in a studio adjoining the temple. This disquieting Taoist shrine, not far from the airport at BAYAN LEPAS, is included on round-island tours and easily reached by bus.

Nothing on Penang is as charming as its **kampongs,** which are meticulously neat in forest or seaside settings. The most picturesque of these traditional elevated villages is

Left: Taking the air in a Penang kampong's typically spotless house.
Right: Oddly, some nights all the snakes vacate the temple precincts.

strung out along the new Jalan Bharu road. Other *kampongs* worth visiting are BALIK PULAU and PULAU BETONG. You can be sure you'll be welcomed warmly.

Penang's most beautiful shoreline lies north at the **Batu Ferringhi** hotel strip of palm-studded coves and beaches. But the cleanest swimming is south past the airport around **Batu Maung** and **Gertak Sanggul** and also at the isolated beach extending toward Muka Head Lighthouse in the far north-west beyond TELOK BAHANG.

The **Batik Factory** and **Butterfly Farm** just south of Telok Bahang are sights well worth

Honeymooners flock to Batu Ferringhi, one of Malaysia's most popular beaches.

visiting and should be included in any round-the-island tour.

Good scuba diving awaits you off the south coast at RIMAU ISLAND (Pulau Rimau).

Better still is the booming resort of LANGKAWI, largest of a group of 99 Malaysian islands and islets about 100 kilometres north of Penang, accessible by air and ferry.

65

Bali

Asia's most fabled isle lies about 1,600 kilometres southeast of Singapore, an easy flight along the great Indonesian archipelago. As you glide in to land, you'll probably see flying fish leaping from the lagoon and Balinesian outriggers moving under brilliantly coloured sails. A law prohibits new buildings from rising higher than the palm trees, which fringe sandy shores as advertised. Behind them a lush, irregular landscape of green ravines, hilly gardens and rice terraces rises towards distant Mount Agung, at 3,142 metres the highest peak on this volcanic island and revered as the home of Bali's gods.

There may be no spot on earth with more beauty—human, natural and artistic. Though nine times the size of Singapore, Bali is smaller than many of Indonesia's thousands of islands. Measuring about 5,000 square kilometres, it's home to about three million gentle, cocoa-skinned people who don't force their flashing smiles.

Since discovery by jetliner tourism, Balinesians have been quick to adopt the commercialism presumed to appeal to visitors. Yet despite increasing encroachments of the modern world, they continue to pursue the old way of life with its traditional religion, art, *gamelan* music, dance and spirit of community.

The best of Bali is not always readily visible. In the most unexpected places you'll find stone and wood carvings, paintings and tiny altars adorned with daily offerings to spirits. Many of the villages and 20,000 temples are deep in tropical vegetation.

Performances staged for tourists—a recent, abnormal phenomenon—are less rewarding than authentic, non-commercial renditions of the mesmerizing all-male *kechak* (monkey) dance, the classical *legong* dance by agile preadolescent girls and the wildly energetic *barong* demon dance.

The more you explore, the more you'll succumb to the charm of the island. Even on a brief holiday, don't fail to leave the beach and head inland. That's where the magic is.

Island Sights

From Bali's beach hotel areas, Kuta, Sanur and Nusa Dua, agencies conduct daily minibus or private car tours, which aren't always as instructive as could be wished. To mix with the people (and save money), take the *bemos*, small vehicles which

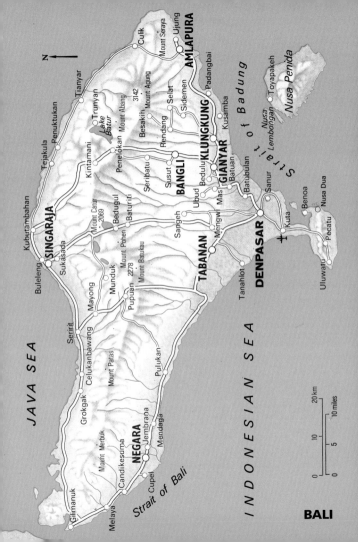

BALI

go almost everywhere. Taxi rates, controlled only on the airport route, can be crippling elsewhere—unless you're firm. You can always hire a car or motorbike and join the motorized legions clogging Bali's underdeveloped roads.

However you travel, you will probably pass through DENPASAR, the noisy, traffic-jammed, disorderly capital. Make a *morning* visit to the sprawling central market. Sarong-clad shoppers haggle here, while small girls carry huge loads on their heads.

Denpasar's **Museum** displays a sampling of Bali's unique artistic heritage in three small buildings around a central courtyard. Don't fail to see the jewelled *krises*, 15th-century double-edged daggers with elaborate handles said to house the souls of their bravest owners. The other-worldly dance masks and costumes and the wall calendar showing earthquake predictions and auspicious days for religious ceremonies are also worth

Bali's incomparable rice terraces. **69**

seeing. Look for the model of the spectacular cremation ceremony you'll probably come across on the island. There are also outstanding wood carvings from village temples. These were used in the teeth-filing ritual still practiced on young girls.

It's a rare day without at least one temple festival somewhere on Bali. (Typically, most islanders know precisely how many days it is until festivals months ahead, but will be vague about their own birth dates.) Watching these spectacles, you'll appreciate the complexity of the animistic religion so central to this island culture.

Besakih, the "Mother Temple", sprawls far above the picturesque Bukit Jambul rice terraces and is high on the slopes of the holy Mount Agung volcano. The most dramatic ceremonies occur here, some 60 kilometres north of Denpasar. Long dormant, Agung erupted violently in 1963, the year of Bali's greatest, once-in-a-century purification rites. You won't convince many Balinesians that the deaths of over a thousand people were coincidence. It's easy to believe in angry gods as you look out from the terraced Besakih complex, studded with black-tiered *merus* (roofs). The view is as awesome as the size of offerings balanced on the heads of female pilgrims.

Very different scenery is the attraction at **Uluwatu** on the arid southern tableland, where an impressive grey stone temple perches on a sheer cliff overhanging the sea.

Holy snakes snooze in caves beneath the limestone outcropping of another seaside temple at **Tanahlot** on the south-western coast. The temple, which is reached on foot during low

70

tide, is hardly worth the long, jolting ride on atrocious roads. But the rural scenes along the way are memorable: ducks parading down rice paddies in perfect formation; communal streams for the washing of humans, animals and motorbikes; cows guided by children carrying smaller brothers and sisters; and elderly ladies with black-ened teeth and shrivelled faces who haven't heard that Bali's traditional toplessness has long since been taboo in the era of tourism.

The large, moat-enclosed temple complex at **Mengwi** has exceptional stone carvings, frequent cockfights and a promised museum and information centre. Nobody will ob-

Balinesians by the thousands worship at Besakih, the holiest shrine.

ject if you peek through the open windows of the primary schools close by.

Another terrible road leads on to the picturesque **Monkey Forest** at SANGEH. Here grey monkeys, often too blasé about tourist handouts to bother with your peanuts, wander around the mossy, intricately carved Bukit Sari temple, which is sur-

rounded by acres of extremely tall *pala* trees.

Exotic rock reliefs decorate the entrance to the **Elephant Cave** near BEDULU. Inside this former Buddhist monastery you can see the T-shaped niches where the monks once slept. The main shrine of the large **Kehen Temple** in BANGLI boasts the maximally sacred 11

Left: Elephant Cave's mysteries are not all solved. Right: Children are awed by hilarious monster in barong *dance, a traditional spectacle.*

merus. In the first courtyard there's a wooden temple bell in a fabulous banyan tree with many trunks said to be 300 years old.

The "aboriginal" Bali Aga village of TRUNYAN is, regardless of much local promotion, a disappointment. The choppy trip by small boat across Lake Batur in the north is reasonably scenic. There are good mountain, lake and lava-flow views from PENELOKAN and KINTAMANI.

Swimming is quite good off the long, sandy beach at KUTA, where surfing is often appealing. You'll find a youthful crowd and bungalow-style accommodations here. SANUR's large, high-rise hotels are more expensive. The water is too shallow for comfortable swimming, and currents can be tricky out towards the reef. NUSA DUA, south of Kuta, is a new resort development, very complete in facilities, and respectful of environment.

What to Do

Shopping

Shopping in Singapore is little short of sensational. The variety of shops and merchandise may seem bewildering, but prices are most satisfying. Raffles, after all, founded this as a free port. Today that means you can purchase a great many items duty free.

Air-conditioned, multi-storied shopping centres are all the rage, especially in the tourist hotel area. But Singapore still has hundreds of small shops. In addition to department stores, some of them Japanese, there are Chinese emporiums jammed with inexpensive mainland products. Leading hotels have their own shopping arcades, displaying the elegant merchandise you won't find in Chinatown.

Perhaps because they imagine tourists like to sleep late, most shopkeepers don't open their businesses until about 10 a.m. But you can continue shopping until 9.30 or 10 at night, even on Sundays and holidays in many cases. Don't miss the night market *(pasar malam)* held Wednesday, Saturday and Sunday evenings at the Singapore Handicrafts Centre in Tanglin Road.

Singapore Shopping Sense

Know what you are looking for and how much you would pay for it at home. You may not always get expert advice, and sales staff are not necessarily trained in their specific line. Thus they may try to sell you what they *think* you want and not what you really want.

Unless you're in a big hurry, always compare prices before you buy. First visit department stores where prices are fixed, then go to shops and boutiques where prices are negotiable. The farther from the Orchard Road hotel district and central shopping area you go, the less you should pay, although the selection may be limited.

Whatever you're thinking of buying, automatically ask for a discount. You'll usually be given one just as automatically. Japanese goods may be rou-

Elegant boutiques simply aren't making any inroads in Chinatown.

tinely discounted by as much as 40 per cent. Reputable stores will produce price lists for electrical appliances, cameras and watches.

Don't hesitate to bargain. Forget any embarrassment: this is universally accepted practice in Singapore.

Be sure to inspect and test before you pay. Find out if your electrical goods will need a transformer for the voltage back home. Singapore shops rarely refund money, but they'll often exchange what you've bought.

Don't fail to obtain an internationally valid guarantee or warranty for such purchases as watches, cameras and electrical appliances. A genuine warranty card (forgeries accompany smuggled, reconditioned-like-new or imitation goods), carries the manufacturer's or agent's name. Most dealers display a copy of an official warranty card.

Your receipt, essential for customs declarations, should state item, brand, model, serial number, date of purchase and price. The carat and percentage of precious metal should appear on jewellery receipts. When a shop undertakes to mail purchases abroad, they should include delivery details on a letter-headed receipt.

If you're travelling on to Hong Kong, note that knowledgeable Singaporeans shop there for locally made leather handbags, shoes, clothing and toys.

Beware of touts, a minor blight on the shopping scene. These people will falsely claim to represent the STPB or your hotel. Well dressed, friendly and illegal, they operate in hotel lobbies, at shopping centres, on guided tours and in restaurants. They specialize in amazing "bargains" at places to which they'll gladly escort you, perhaps throwing in a "free city tour". The bargains will be nothing more than cheap copies of famous brands, smuggled goods or over-priced merchandise.

Consult the STPB list of shops and businesses granted official transfers (decals) as Associate Members "on compliance with certain conditions and regulations which ensure observance of high standards of business ethics". A fee is paid to STPB by each establishment so

Some of the most stunning fabrics are woven by Balinesian girls who demonstrate the techniques of their craft in Singapore.

Duty-Free Shopping
Except at the airport, no "tax-free" or "duty-free" signs are allowed in Singapore, since that advantage applies everywhere. The following goods are sold duty-free in the island republic:

- Antiques (items more than a century old)
- Calculators
- Cameras
- Carpets
- Carved ivory and mother-of-pearl
- Jewellery
- Leather (except clothing and its accessories)
- Lighters
- Musical instruments
- Pearls
- Pens
- Perfume and cosmetics
- Precious and semi-precious stones
- Radios
- Record players
- Shavers
- Silk (except ready-made garments and accessories)
- Spectacles (glasses)
- Tape recorders
- Toys
- Typewriters
- Watches
- Wigs

Note that the only duty-free spirits (liquor), perfume and tobacco products are sold at the airport.

listed. There are many reputable places to shop in Singapore.

Best Buys
Singapore offers a wide range of merchandise:

Antiques include Chinese jade, ceramics, bronzes, scrolls, gowns, incense burners and snuff bottles; Thai ceramics and bronzes; Annamese porcelain; Indian brass; and Indonesian wooden masks and carvings. Beware of fakes, buy only in reputable shops and ask for a certificate of authenticity.

Batik is an ancient Middle-Eastern fabric-printing craft now associated with Indonesia, Malaysia and Singapore. You'll see *batik* sarongs, dresses, skirts and shirts of cotton or voile, as well as *batik* by the metre.

Carpets of both antique and modern design are for sale from China, Persia, India, Pakistan and Singapore itself.

Curios and **handwork** are on display from around Asia at the Singapore Handicraft Centre in Tanglin Road. Native demonstrators, such as Balinesian woodcarvers and *songket* weavers, are interesting to watch, even if you're not buying. Look out for Indian sandalwood figurines and fans. You'll find Ceylonese gemstones and ebony elephants. Filigreed silver and *mengkuang* leaf hats and mats from Malaysia are unusual, as well as ornaments of seashell, tortoise and coconut.

Electronic equipment and **cameras.** Shops carry the very latest models.

Jade comes primarily from Burma and is beloved above all stones by the Chinese*. In its natural state it is white, but "impurities" may make it green (the most expensive colour), red, black, yellow or lavender. Jade is expensive even in Singapore, but worth knowledgeable buying. Less pricey substitutes like aventurine, serpentine and rose quartz ("pink jade") are popular.

Jewellery of gold, often intricately worked, is sold at South Bridge Road and People's Park shopping complex. You'll also see South African diamonds, Burmese rubies, Japanese pearls and Malaysian silver.

Orchids in mixed sprays can be air-freighted abroad in boxes or carried with you, and gold-plated "Risis" orchids make unusual jewellery.

---

* Confucius said of Jade: "Flaws do not hide its excellence, nor its excellence flaws, suggesting loyalty. It has an internal radiance, like good faith. Bright as a brilliant rainbow, it resembles Heaven".

Malaysian pewter, notably Selangor ware, is produced in Singapore and considered the world's finest. Some of the pewter objects on sale have modern teak handles and bases and an attractive hand-hammered finish. Known as "white pewter", Malaysia's product contains no lead, just 97 per cent tin and 3 per cent antimony and copper. Caring for lead-free pewter is easy, since it doesn't tarnish. Pewterware should not be any cheaper in Malaysia than here.

You can see local artisans demonstrating pewter techniques at the Selangor Pewter showroom in Alexandra Road. It's fascinating to watch them hammering the pewterware and hand polishing it with leaves—the secret of its satin-smooth finish.

Reptile skin goods are by world standards reasonably priced here and beautifully made. Crocodiles, particularly salt-water species (on display before and after at a "farm", see p. 48), provide the most admired skins for bags, shoes, wallets, belts and accessories. You'll also see articles in alligator, snake and lizard.

Silk, hugely popular, is used in Chinese *cheongsams,* Indian saris, pieces of gold-embroidered *kain songket* from Kelantan in Malaysia and distinctive neckties from Thailand.

Tailor-made clothing can be had in 24 hours, but try to allow a few days for fittings on a Malay *sarong kebaya* of *batik* and lace, an Indian silk or chiffon sari, or a *cheongsam* of silk or brocade with high collar and ankle-to-thigh side slits. For men, safari jackets and suits are Singapore specialities.

Souvenirs and **small gifts** are peddled by Chinatown hawk-

Consumer electronics, cameras, cassettes... the shopping is satisfying in Singapore.

ers, who sell chopsticks, umbrellas, hand fans, good luck scrolls, wooden clogs, sandalwood statuettes, paper lanterns, incense burners, mahjong tiles and bamboo back-scratchers. If Peking, Hong Kong or Taiwan aren't on your itinerary, Chinese emporiums like People's Park offer dozens of items, such as calligraphy brushes and Chinese potions, which are both portable and inexpensive. Bangles, cheesecloth blouses, silver curios, spices and peacock feathers are available in the Serangoon Road "Little India" area. Or perhaps you'd fancy a T-shirt lettered in Chinese, Tamil or Malay script.

Shopping on Penang

Because rents and other overheads for shops are lower than in Singapore, shopping in George Town for foreign luxury goods might be worthwhile. Certainly spirits and tobacco products are vastly cheaper than in heavily taxed Singapore. Specially licensed George Town stores sell such duty-free items as cameras, radios and watches. The Tourist Development Corporation has a duty-free shop in the Tun Abdul Razak Complex on Penang Road, the main shopping street, where you can buy spirits and cigarettes.

Note that your duty-free purchases cannot be used in Penang. They will be delivered to you at the airport. If you're going overland through Malaysia, you must present half of a two-part receipt at customs.

Shop for everyday basics and local crafts at the colourful *pasar malam*, the movable night stall market.

Shopping on Bali

Most of Indonesia's shopping bargains are to be found in Bali. There is a government-operated handicraft centre five kilometres to the east of Denpasar, the Sanggraha Kriya Asta, where Bali's best buys are gathered under one roof: wood carvings and paintings, as well as gold and silver objects and jewellery and traditional weaving.

For buyers and browsers, **Ubud** is the leading centre of Balinesian painting; you can visit artists at work in their studios or carry home a painting from one of the town's galleries. You'll find the best wood carvers in **Mas,** busily crafting the objects you'll see on sale in village shops. You may need expert help to distinguish the authentic works of art from the mass-produced objects seen everywhere.

81

Sports

With physical fitness something of an officially approved mania, particularly among young Singaporeans, both sports facilities and joggers abound. Early morning is wisest for outdoor sports, as exertion in the equatorial heat has humbled many a visitor. You can bowl or play table-tennis in air-conditioned comfort if you wish. For spectators there are frequent games of soccer, rugby and field hockey on the Padang opposite City Hall and horse racing at the Singapore Turf Club off Dunearn Road.

Tennis and Squash. Booming in popularity, racquet sports are easily accessible to tourists. There's even a daily tennis tour with bus service from hotels. Courts and equipment may be rented inexpensively. Most courts are illuminated at night. Booking is easier during the week.

Golf. In addition to Sentosa's attractive golf courses, Singapore has numerous installations on the main island which are open to non-members. You can arrange to play through your hotel. Clubs may be hired. Caddies, not carts, are the rule here. Greens fees are higher at weekends.

Whether it's strenuous action on the links or lazing at the pool, don't under-rate the torrid sun.

Water Sports. Most visitors will probably prefer to forego swimming while in Singapore, except perhaps in their hotel pool. There is an artificial swimming lagoon on Sentosa, and the east coast area and several southern islands have been developed for bathing.

Snorkelling and **scuba diving** are not very rewarding. You should see some fish, coral and a wreck or two around Sisters Island, Kusu, Pulau Hantu and Raffles Lighthouse. Go with a local expert and beware of tricky currents. Farther afield, there is excellent diving at Malaysia's Tioman and Rawa islands.

At Ponggol Point you can hire skis and a boat to **water-ski** in the Johore Strait. It's usually placid. **Deep-sea fishing** is not easily arranged, but you can cast your line into fresh-water lakes near Changi.

Flying. Visitors with a full pilot's licence can rent a Cessna, Piper or Twin Comanche by the hour (cheaper on weekdays) at Seletar Airfield's Singapore Flying Club. The aerial view of the harbour is unforgettable.

83

Entertainment

Though hardly "swinging" by current international standards, Singapore offers a varied after-dark scene with enough exotica to keep most visitors amused. Much the best and cheapest is to mingle with local families at outdoor food stalls where you can have supper until late at night. This is one aspect of the real Singapore that no bulldozer will sweep away. (A selection of food stalls convenient to tourist hotels appears on page 94.)

Unfortunately, prices on the formal entertainment circuit generally range from high to outrageous, even if you drink nothing alcoholic. They reflect the high fees paid to name performers, Western and Asian. Much of the action is in the larger hotels, which have nightclubs, discotheques, cocktail lounges and a few regional cultural shows.

The city has a handful of theatre-restaurants and **cabarets** attended by families and couples until about 10 p.m. When they depart, swarms of male customers book and pay for "hostesses" of their choice by the hour, for drinking and dancing on the premises or social companionship else-where. This familiar Asian ritual is also played out at various drink-dance lounges. It somehow seems sedate, rather than sinful, a faint echo of Singapore's bawdy old days.

Crashing cymbals and gongs will alert you to one of the rare outdoor operas performed on the streets by **wayang** troupes,

until television the island's best-loved entertainers. In these exaggerated dramatizations of ancient Chinese legends, you'll catch the drift without knowing the dialect: the heroes wear red or green, an emperor yellow and the villains black. Admission is free to *wayangs,* which often last for hours. Take your camera.

Through the year Singapore sees a reasonable sprinkling of international musical ensembles and soloists who give **concerts** and **recitals,** so that you might hear something you

Chinese ensemble performing the Lotus Dance.

missed at home. The Singapore Symphony Orchestra performs every fortnight.

The Singapore Cultural Theatre in Grange Road is the venue for **musicals, jazz** and **pop** events.

Singaporeans are among the world's greatest movie-goers. The average citizen sees 19 films per year, despite censorship, according to United Nations reports. The island has over 50 air-conditioned **cinemas,** all inexpensive. They're jammed on week-ends, so book ahead. English subtitles appear on eastern-style westerns, featuring sampans and swords instead of rifles and covered wagons.

From time to time exhibitions of ancient **Chinese martial arts** are staged, as unusual as anything you'll see in Singapore. Kung-fu masters chop bricks without breaking the fresh eggs they're standing on. They turn chopsticks and playing cards into lethal weapons and repel spear thrusts with their bare necks.

For visitors who'd like a quick dose of Chinese, Indian and Malay pageantry, the Tourist Board promotes the **"Instant Asia" Cultural Show.** You'll see everything from folk dances to snake charmers (at **86** Raffles Hotel on Beach Road).

Festivals

Whenever you visit the multicultural Republic, there should be some sort of festivity to see and photograph. Major celebrations are in rough chronological order. Dates vary except where noted. Christian holidays such as Good Friday and Christmas are also observed in Singapore.

Chinese New Year. This 15-day lunar festival in late January or early February is Singapore's biggest blow-out. After copious feasting and lively celebrations during the first two days, everyone turns out for the spectacular Chingay Parade. There are lion and dragon dancers, acrobats, jugglers and stilt walkers. The din of drums and cymbals has replaced the traditional fireworks, now banned for safety reasons. On the last night, *chap goh mei*, when the moon is full, there's another big family feast and many Chinese pray to the "Queen of Heaven" at the old Wak Cheng Bio in Phillips Street. Young ladies traditionally consider this night auspicious for romance and husband-hunting.

Thaipusam (January/February). In this remarkable, if gruesome, Hindu festival, devotees of Lord Subramaniam skewer their bodies, which are decorated with fruit, flowers and peacock feathers, and parade chanting from Perumal Temple in Serangoon Road to Chettiar Temple in Tank Road.

Birthday of the Monkey God (16th–17th days of first moon). Piercing of cheeks and tongues, this time by Chinese spirit mediums, and street processions mark this celebration honouring Tai Seng Yeh, the Monkey God, believed to cure the sick and absolve the hopeless. This popular deity, the godfather of many Chinese children, has a second annual festival in autumn.

Mouludden Nabi (Prophet Mohammed's birthday). The largest celebration of this Muslim holiday is at the Sultan

There are many ways of having a swinging time at the Chingay Parade.

Mosque in North Bridge Road, where scholars lecture on Mohammed in Arabic, Tamil, Malay and English.

Birthday of the Saint of the Poor (22nd day of second moon). Still more mediums with skewered flesh accompany the image of the Chinese saint Kong Teck Choon Ong in a colourful procession from White Cloud Temple in Ganges Avenue.

Songkrant Festival (April 13). A joyful water ceremony takes place at Thai Buddhist temples in Silat and Holland Roads, where images of Buddha are bathed and visitors and worshippers sprinkled to welcome the new year.

Birthday of the Third Prince (8th–9th days of fourth moon). This Taoist festival honouring a miracle-making child god features entranced mediums lashing themselves with spiked maces and swords and a procession at North Boat Quay.

Vesak Day. To celebrate Buddha's birth, death and enlightenment, thousands pray and perform good deeds, monks chant *sutras* and candlelight parades are staged at such temples as 1,000 Lights in Race Course Road and Pher Kark See in Bright Hill Drive.

Dragon Boat Festival (5th day of fifth moon). The protest suicide of an ancient Chinese poet-hero who drowned himself is commemorated by boat races held off the Esplanade, interspersed with frog, lion and dragon dances and karate demonstrations.

National Day (August 9). Highlight of National Day is the military parade; dancers, musicians and acrobats fill the city green, the Padang, in celebration of Singapore's independence in 1965.

Hari Raya Puasa (1st day of the tenth month of the Muslim calendar). Merrymaking, feasting and thanksgiving prayers celebrate the end of Ramadan, the Muslim month of fasting, in this biggest of Malay festivals.

Festival of the Hungry Ghosts (seventh moon). Banquets given by stallholders, Chinese street opera, puppet shows and ritual burning of incense and mock riches appease the spirits who wander free of purgatory at this time each year.

Navarathri Festival (Sept./Oct.). Nine days of prayer, temple music and classical dances honour the consorts of Siva, Vishnu and Brahma (the Hindu trinity of Gods), notably

From martial arts to opera, Singapore's Chinese perpetuate their ancestral traditions.

at the Chettiar Hindu Temple, Tank Road, ending with a procession on the tenth day.

Moon Cake Festival (15th day of eighth moon). On this night, when the moon is said to be roundest and brightest, Chinese children parade with elaborate candlelit lanterns and eat moon cakes filled with lotus-seed paste, duck egg yolks and sugared winter melon.

Festival of the Nine Emperor Gods (1st–9th days of ninth moon). Street operas and processions for nine days honour these nine deities who cure ailments and bring wealth and longevity to Chinese believers.

Pilgrimage to Kusu Island (ninth moon). During the month some 100,000 Taoists take boats to this sacred southern island to picnic, leave offerings and pray for prosperity, health and obedient children.

Thimithi Festival (October). After a procession from the Perumal Temple in Serangoon

Road, Hindu devotees in a partial trance walk over burning embers at the Sri Mariamman Temple in South Bridge Road, fulfilling vows to a goddess.

Deepavali (Oct./Nov.). Every Hindu home is lighted and brightly decorated, people wear new clothes, and shrines are swamped with offerings to celebrate the ancient Festival of Lights, a major Indian holiday marking the victory of light over darkness.

Hari Raya Haji (10th day of 12th month of Muslim calendar). Prayers at mosques and the sacrificial slaughter of goats and cows for distribution to the needy mark this Muslim festival of special significance for Mecca pilgrims.

Left: Dragon boatmen strain. Right: Thaipusam is not for the squeamish.

Dining

The most exciting eating experience in Asia awaits you in Singapore. It's possible to dine twice a day for months without repeating a dish. And what dishes! Ten Chinese cuisines, North and South Indian, Malay-Indonesian, indigenous Nonya, Thai, Japanese and Korean are all utterly authentic. There's also very respectable European fare and even (if you must), American fast food.

Your most difficult decisions will be where and what to eat. Proper restaurants range from revolving affairs on top of tall buildings to informal places where you eat from banana leaves under ceiling fans. Various 24-hour coffee houses produce 50 or more dishes. Some of Singapore's greatest food is served at hotel restaurants. And some of the worst (ask around as everybody knows).

Restaurants are open from noon to 3 and 7 to 11 p.m. at least. Booking is often necessary at the best spots, since gourmet dining, usually in large groups, is a popular pastime. For wedding parties,

Meticulous chopping of everything from glazed duck to sugared spare ribs is basic Chinese kitchen art. **93**

birthdays and business reunions, dining rooms or entire restaurants are reserved.

At places where service is not included on the bill, don't be annoyed if the waiter or waitress appears anxious for a tip. This is handed over here as soon as the change is brought, a no-nonsense custom diners don't seem to mind.

Food Stalls

An entire Singapore holiday can be spent eating outdoors. Your meals will be superb and surprisingly cheap. A tradition dating back to Raffles, open air food stalls may change places or be spruced up now and then, but otherwise they've survived "progress" intact.

Despite their simple, often chaotic appearance, the stalls are clean places to eat. Government health inspectors make sure of that. There's nothing hidden away in the kitchen. You choose what you see and watch it being prepared. Cooking here is quicker and less elaborate than in restaurants, but no less imaginative or delicious. Some of the tastiest dishes are found only, or mainly, at hawker stalls: *Hokkien fried mee, popiah, or luah* and *bubo cha cha,* for example. You can simultaneously sample Chinese, Malay and Indian specialities. And it's easy to keep going back for more.

The procedure is simple: find an empty table, note its number or position and wander about inspecting the stalls and ordering what you'd like (not necessarily what the friendliest hawker is dishing up). You're not obliged to buy anything from the stall nearest to your table. Signs in English list the specialities and prices of each hawker, who will serve each dish when it's ready.

Always thronged with Singaporeans, hawker stalls relatively convenient to hotels include those at Newton Circus, Rasa Singapura (behind Tanglin Road Handicraft Centre), Kreta Ayer (at Smith and Tregganu streets), Cuppage Road, People's Park, Empress Place and Satay Club (facing the sea on Queen Elizabeth Walk). Some are open during the day and others at night. All are inexpensive.

Chinese Cuisines

Of the world's two greatest cuisines, French may be more sophisticated but Chinese is infinitely more varied. In Singapore you can eat your way through almost every Chinese cooking style. Restaurants usually specialize in one regional cuisine.

It's clearly preferable to eat Chinese food in a group, tasting a number of dishes set out for general consumption with individual bowls of rice and soup. A "small" portion is fine for two or three diners. When you're pondering menus which often list several hundred dishes, don't overlook vegetables, which can be more spectacular than many seafood, meat and poultry courses. After all, Chinese chefs invented the *nouvelle cuisine* treatment of certain vegetables centuries ago. Mushrooms are also a speciality.

The fragrance and colour of the dishes are as intoxicating as the taste. Other than the ubiquitous soya sauce, distinctive Chinese seasonings include sesame, oyster, chilli, black, yellow or red bean, garlic, ginger and black vinegar.

You'll agree food tastes better with chopsticks. There's no secret to using them; several hundred million children do it daily. In fact, chopstick techniques vary slightly. With a little practice you'll avoid starvation. Note that it's perfectly in order to raise your bowl close to your mouth when chopsticking rice.

Local people often order soft drinks or beer instead of the tea that is automatically served.

Among the pleasures of a Chinese meal is the hot or cold perfumed towel you're given before and after dining.

Szechuan. Spicier and heartier than most Chinese food, Szechuan cuisine is enjoyed by a growing number of connoisseurs. The traditionally liberal use of hot red peppers is supposedly a protection against cold and disease in the mountainous western province. *Szechuan fried rice*, which can be magnificent, balances spicy dishes.

You may find *smoked Szechuan duck* to be the most delicious dish in Singapore, even better than the more famous Peking version. Szechuan chefs smoke the duck in tea leaves and camphor sawdust. The skin is crisp. It's served in pieces, which you dip into a dark, sweet soya and Chinese liquor sauce.

Not even the natives normally eat the dried red chillis in *diced chicken with pepper*, a spicy dish. *Szechuan chilli prawns* are served in a slightly sweet garlic sauce. Other dishes representative of this cuisine are *minced pork with bean curd, pork leg in brown sauce, steamed chicken in lotus leaves, fried eels in garlic sauce* and *Szechuan sour soup*.

Peking. Down through the

dynasties Imperial chefs refined this great cuisine which, though northern, embraces all Chinese regional kitchens. Dumplings, noodles and steamed buns predominate since wheat is the staple, but in Singapore rice may also accompany the meal.

Peking duck, an internationally known delicacy, is rather expensive but worth it. The roasted duck meat and crisp skin are sliced and wrapped up in a rice pancake with spring onions and cucumber in a dark, sweet sauce. Some of the duck may be cooked separately with bean sprouts. The bones and salted vegetables can make a soup.

Shi choy, fresh, deep-fried bamboo shoots, are smothered in crisp, shredded and slightly sweet green vegetables. *Hot and sour soup* is a dark, piquant blend of various vegetables. *Shredded beef with green peppers*, often with spring onions, and *fried scallop and kale*, attest to the mastery of Peking chefs. *Drunken chicken*, a typical cold appetizer, is marinated in rice wine. *Mashed-bean egg*, deep-fried whipped egg white stuffed with red beans, is one of many unusual Peking sweets.

Cantonese. Emigrants from Canton have made this the best known Chinese cuisine in the world. Although frogs, pigeons and snakes may find their way into the cooking pot, Cantonese seasoning is mild. You'll notice the lighter soya sauce and much root ginger. *Dim sum*, a Cantonese invention usually available only at lunch time here, is a mobile buffet. You choose from steamed, stuffed dumplings and other titbits brought around on trolleys.

Foremost among Cantonese specialities is *shark's fin*, a costly delicacy beloved by most Chinese. The fin is boiled, thinly shredded and usually served in a crab, chicken or corn soup. It may also come mixed with scrambled egg or in a bowl on its gelatinous own *(pow chee)*. Fried bean sprouts are the usual accompaniment. Order *Buddha jumps over the wall* and you'll be served a soup of shark's fin, abalone, sea cucumber and seven other ingredients, steamed in a sealed ceramic bowl for half a day.

Hundred-year-old eggs look ancient because they have been preserved for about a month in ash, lime, clay and tea leaves, which turn the egg white black and the yolk greenish-grey. Duck eggs are treated in this way and make an interesting appetizer, served with pickled ginger and pickled leeks. *Bird's nest* is a rare and expensive treat reserved for special occasions. The translucent threads of swifts' nests are served in soup or cooked with chicken breast.

Three delicacies is just that: fish, prawn and sea cucumber, stewed together. *Mah mee* combines soupy spaghetti with prawns, fish, pork and greens. In *chee cheong fun*, flat noodles are wrapped around prawns, chicken or mushrooms, with oyster sauce, sesame oil and grated fried garlic. Cantonese chefs marinate pieces of chicken in ginger juice and wine, deep-fry them and serve the *paper chicken* in grease-proof paper.

Hokkien. Since Marco Polo probably brought the secret of pasta back to Italy from China, it's not surprising that Chinese chefs are noodle masters. Par-

At Newton Circus and other great food stall complexes the choice of tempting dishes is incredible.

ticularly the Hokkiens. Look for them at the hawker stalls, as there are very few Hokkien restaurants. Specialities include *Hokkien fried (prawn) mee,* moist noodles with prawn, squid, pork, bean sprouts and other vegetables, also served in soup. *Or chien* (also *or luah*) is a seasoned omelet with tiny oysters and spring onions.

Prawns with satay are cooked to perfection both in Singapore and on Penang. Prawns are grilled, shelled and served in a rather spicy sauce of pineapple, spring onions and herbs. The Hokkien chefs also make excellent *bah kut teh,* a soup of pork ribs, garlic and herbs.

Eight-jewel chicken, which is steamed and boned, is stuffed with diced pork, mushrooms, dried prawns, carrots and glutinous rice. Carrot cake, an omelet-like affair, features grated radish (called "white carrot" by the Chinese). Other Hokkien staples are *hay cho,* deep-fried balls of prawn, mashed pork and water chestnuts; *popiah,* a rice-flour spring roll of turnip, bamboo shoot, bean sprouts, bean curd, prawn, shredded meat and garlic; and *or leong,* deep-fried mashed sweet potato.

Teochew. Seafood is the basis of this light, non-greasy southern cuisine. The fresh fish is sweet because it's first mixed with sweet berry sauce, peanuts and sesame oil. Try *steamboat,* the Teochew version of fondue. Pieces of fish and seafood, meat, chicken and vegetables are dipped by each diner into hot stock in the "steamboat".

The favourite hawker-stall noodle dish is *char kway teow,* with prawns, clams, bean sprouts and eggs fried in a spicy, dark soya sauce. *Chilli crab,* a Singaporean standby, is crab fried with a sauce of ginger, garlic and chillis.

Shanghainese. Seafood dominates this cuisine and many dishes are stewed in dark soya. Specialities are *braised fish heads* or *tails, fried noodles* with shrimps and chive shoots, *braised abalone* in sesame sauce, *fried eels* and *crab and sweet corn soup.*

Hainanese. This southern Chinese island's great contribution is perhaps Singapore's most delectable chicken dish: *Hainanese chicken rice.* The chicken is stuffed with ginger, boiled and served in pieces with garlic-flavoured rice and a special sauce of pounded chillis, lime and chicken fat. *Mutton soup,* also typical, is simmered with Chinese herbs, ginger and young bamboo shoots.

Taiwanese. For those who like their rice wet, it comes in porridge with sweet potato chunks at the city's several Taiwanese restaurants, a bland complement to such piquant dishes as *pork, bean curd and brown bean paste; cockles and mussels* in chilli-bean paste or black soya sauce and *kangkong*, a leafy green vegetable fried with chilli paste.

Hakka. This basic southern cuisine uses lots of sweet potato and dried shrimp. Sample *yong tau foo*, deep-fried bean curd, chillis and other vegetables stuffed with fish paste and *mui choy*, a pickled spinach-like vegetable cooked with pork.

Hunanese. Starting to make an impact in Singapore as elsewhere, this southern cuisine is somewhat less spicy and oily than Szechuan. *Hunan ham*, considered a rare delicacy, is honey-flavoured and served in slices with thinly sliced bread. *Minced pigeon in bamboo tube* and *baked bean curd skin*, wrapped in a pancake like Peking Duck with spring onions and dark sauce, are standard Hunan fare.

Other Cuisines

Elsewhere on the Singapore food scene, you'll find the great **Korean** specialities *bulgogi* and *kimchi;* **Japanese** *tempura, su-*
kiyaki, teppanyaki and *sashimi;* and **Thai** seafood, spicy *tom yam* (sweet and sour soup) and oyster salad. The variety of national dishes seems endless.

Malay. Though overshadowed by the dazzling Chinese gastronomical array, Malay cooking benefits from the more inventive use of coconut milk and all those local spices, herbs and roots. Pork is completely avoided in accordance with Muslim teaching. Generally Malay dishes aren't quite as sizzling as their Indonesian near-cousins.

The best feature of *satay*– beef, chicken, mutton or prawn pieces marinated in sugared spices, skewered and cooked over charcoal—is the gluey accompanying sauce of ground peanuts, peanut oil, chillis, garlic, onion, sugar and tamarind water (the Chinese version includes grated pineapple). Satay comes with cucumber slices, raw onion and glutinous rice chunks *(ketupat)* and is well cooked at the Satay Club.

Mee rebus is a combination of noodles with beef, chicken or prawns and soya bean curd cubes, in a piquant brown gravy. The prawns in *prawn sambal* are very spicy and are served in coconut milk with chillis and crushed lemon leaves. *Tahu goreng*, a soya **99** bean cake in a sweet, spicy peanut sauce with cucumber slices, is served on a nest of bean sprouts. Rice seasoned with lemon grass, chillis, ginger and soya accompanies *beef rendang,* pieces of beef marinated in coconut milk.

Malay *otak otak,* fish paste with coconut and sugar inside cocopalm leaves, differs from the Nonya version, which is grilled in a banana leaf. Bananas are mashed and deep-fried in *jemput jemput,* and *chendol* is an intriguing coconut milk drink, or liquid sweet, with red beans, green jelly and brown sugar.

Indonesian. If you haven't already acquired a taste for hot food, this is not the place to start, although some dishes are only moderately palate-searing. A piquant peanut sauce accompanies *gado gado,* a

In emergencies, there are always hotel buffet lunches where forks and knives outnumber chopsticks.

vegetable, egg and fruit salad. Typical of Indonesian fish dishes are *sotong goreng asam*, fried cuttlefish in sweet black chilli sauce and *udang pepes*, marinated prawns or fish cooked in chilli sauce and coconut milk, wrapped in banana leaves and baked.

Oyor ayam, chicken pieces simmered in spiced coconut gravy, is similar to the more elaborate *Curry Kapitan*. Yellow *nasi lemac*, rice cooked in coconut milk and coloured with turmeric, may come with wildly hot *sambal belachan*, lime juice and chillis pounded with roasted shrimp paste. *Nasi goreng*, a multi-ingredient fried rice, and Indonesian *apokat*, an avocado milkshake, appear on many menus.

Nonya. Aromatic and spicy, this indigenous cuisine is a blend of Chinese and Malay and is named for the traditionally kitchen-skilled women of Straits Chinese ancestry, the Nonyas. Spices, pungent roots, aromatic leaves and fried garlic are used in such complex dishes as *laksa*, noodles and spiced, scented, pounded fish in a richly curried coconut gravy.

Bubo cha cha is a cold (or hot) coconut milk creation with pieces of sweet potato and coloured gelatine cubes. In the Nonya version of *otak otak*, a fish cake on a stick with coconut milk, lemon grass, blue ginger and shallots is grilled in a banana leaf. Soya bean and coconut gravy covers the fried rice noodles in *mee siam*, another speciality.

Indian. To keep Singapore's varied Indian community content, its chefs produce most of the curries and other dishes typical of both the mild northern and spicy southern cooking styles. At simple Indian restaurants, including vegetarian eating houses, you eat with your right hand from freshly washed banana leaves (even the splendid yoghurt).

In *murtabah*, the Indian version of pizza, rice dough is folded over chicken, beef or mutton, onion, eggs and vegetables in a curry gravy. Fried mutton chops are spicy and eaten with mint and tamarind chutney, while *kambing*, mutton soup, is actually a mild stew with mutton pieces on the bone.

Other recommended dishes are *Tandoori chicken*, elaborately marinated and baked in a clay oven; *sag gosht*, mutton cubes cooked in spinach; *nasi beryani*, rice with saffron, nuts and spices; *kashmiri pilau*, fried rice with fruit; and *curry puffs*, a pastry snack filled with minced lamb or beef.

Fruit

There are many popular varieties of tropical fruit available here. *Papaya* is best when pink and has a soft and juicy flesh most enjoyed when eaten chilled, with lime juice. The flesh of the *rambutan*—hairy and red with a sweet white centre—separates entirely from the seed when ripe. The dark purple *mangosteen* is also sweet and white within. Local people adore the spiky *durian*, which is notoriously pungent, but for many visitors hardly worth the enduring odour and excessive expense. The *chiku* is brown-skinned, with a soft, sweet, pear-like flesh, while *starfruit*, usually yellow, is watery and slightly sour. When you order a *mango*, ask for the golden, round and sweet Alphonso imported from India, which is better than other varieties.

The fruit, cut into pieces and sold by street hawkers, is hygienic, carefully prepared and perfectly safe to eat.

Drinks

Freshly squeezed fruit juices, including unusual blends of exotic types, are more refreshing (and often less expensive) than bottled soft drinks, which are also widely sold. A particular favourite is fresh or bottled soya bean juice, a somewhat frothy drink thought to be cooling and nutritious.

Tea is omnipresent. The Chinese variety is usually served hot in glasses without sugar, milk or lemon. Waitresses constantly refill your glass during meals. Beer is quite popular, with European, Australian and local brands available. Wine is very expensive, even Australian varieties, but happily it doesn't complement most local food very well.

Whisky and cognac, avail-

able by the bottle in restaurants, are reserved for special occasions in Singapore. Spirits are generally unappreciated and tea may be used by some to toast a friend. The Mandarin Chinese version of "Cheers" is "*Yam Seng*", which is chanted loudly. Visitors will find the usual international range of spirits at hotels and lounges, the prices in the Orchard Road area often so high as to be temperance-inducing. During the late afternoon, a discount of about 20 per cent is offered at some bars.

The *Singapore Sling*, which has attracted enthusiastic fans and bored critics world-wide since its invention here during World War I, is concocted of gin, cherry brandy, fresh lime juice, Cointreau or Benedictine and possibly bitters and soda.

When the chefs have gone to bed, hungry revellers can find food at Albert Street's late-night stands.

BLUEPRINT for a Perfect Trip

How to Get There

Fares change constantly, so it would be wise to consult an informed travel agent for the latest information about discounts and special deals.

From Great Britain

BY AIR: Flights leave daily from London, stopping en route at destinations which vary according to the day you travel. Main types of fares available are first, club and economy class, and single or return APEX (Advanced Purchase Excursion) fares.

Package Tours: Package holidays, often for quite small groups, offer a wide choice. You can go on a fly/sail cruise to Australia, stopping off at Singapore en route, or book a package which includes dormitory-type accommodation (this is the cheapest type of package, though not yet widely available). Most tours fly to Singapore and then offer cruises, rail or coach trips, or flights to Malaysia, Indonesia, Hong Kong and Bangkok. In fact, almost anything you want to do can be incorporated in a package holiday.

BY SEA: The cruise available from Great Britain, the Sea Princess, stops in Singapore for 40 hours. The QE II world cruise (headquarters in Southampton but originating from New York or Fort Lauderdale) also stops over for 48 hours in Singapore. You can, however, fly to Singapore and embark on cruises around Indonesia and Malaysia and as far away as Hong Kong, Japan, Australia and New Zealand. Packages offering different combinations of stopovers are available. For people with plenty of time, there is a cargo service from Rotterdam, Hamburg or Antwerp three to four times a month.

From North America

BY AIR: Singapore is linked with over 30 American cities and three Canadian ones by daily connecting flights via San Francisco and Los Angeles on the West Coast. One major American carrier has direct flights to Singapore from San Francisco three days a week. Of those cities that offer connecting flights, New York, Houston and Toronto have the widest choice of departure times. In addition, another dozen American cities and five cities in Canada offer connecting service on three or more days a week. Fares (in addition to first, club and economy class) available are the Transpacific APEX and the Transpacific Super APEX.

Charter Flights and Package Tours: Singapore is featured on GITs (Group Inclusive Tours) of 15 days or longer to the Far East. Included in these are jet transport, transport from point to point on the itinerary, transfers to and from all airports, hotel accommodations, sightseeing and the services of a qualified guide, most meals, tips and service charges, as well as musical and folk entertainment. These tours for the most part follow a "circle route" and visit Japan, Taiwan, Hong Kong, Thailand, Australia, New Zealand, Fiji and Tahiti, in addition to Singapore. Those who prefer the western route will visit Nepal and India. Several extensions, usually four days in length, are permitted for a slight additional cost. The most popular of these have been to Hawaii and Japan.

BY SEA: From New York and Fort Lauderdale, two cruises (the Sagafjord and Vistafjord of Cunard Lines) set sail to this region. Their four-month itinerary from January to April includes a brief stopover here.

When to Go

Being only 85 miles north of the Equator, the weather is usually sunny with no distinct hot or cold season. However, most rainfall occurs during the north-east Monsoon (November to January). Showers are usually sudden and heavy but also brief and refreshing, although humidity is uncomfortably high at this time of year.

The following charts should give you an idea of the average monthly temperatures in Singapore, and the number of rainy days per month:

		J	F	M	A	M	J	J	A	S	O	N	D
Temperature	°F	79	81	81	81	81	81	81	81	81	81	81	79
	°C	26	27	27	27	27	27	27	27	27	27	27	26
Days of rain		16	11	14	15	14	14	13	14	13	16	20	22

Planning Your Budget

The Singapore experienced by most visitors is costlier than they expected. The upsurge in the tourist sector is much higher than the official inflation rate. The following list of *average* prices tourists will encounter is in Singapore dollars (S$).

Airport. Taxi to Orchard Road hotels about S$11, plus S$2 surcharge (no surcharge for journey from city to airport). Airport departure tax to Brunei and Malaysia S$5, other destinations S$12.

Buses. 40–80 cents depending on distance (flat fees charged on some).

Car hire. *Nissan Sunny 1.3* S$85 per day, 45 cents per kilometre S$110–120 per day with unlimited mileage (within Singapore only). *Datsun Bluebird 1.6* S$105 per day, 60 cents per km., S$130–150 per day with unlimited mileage.

Guides (STPB-licenced). English-speaking S$45 for a 4-hour organized tour, other languages S$85. Personal guide (3 hours minimum period), English-speaking S$120, other languages S$150–170. (Call STPB one day in advance.)

Hairdressers. *Man's* haircut S$15, shampoo S$20. *Woman's* haircut S$20, shampoo and blow-dry S$25, permanent wave S$35.

Hotels (published rates). *Budget range:* single room S$50, double rooms S$55–60. *Mid-range:* single S$120–140, double S$150–190. *Luxury:* single S$200–230, double S$230–290. 3% government tax charged in hotels with more than 50 rooms. 10% service charge added at most hotels. Owing to a glut of rooms, rates are subject to negotiation.

Meals and drinks. Full hotel breakfast S$15, restaurant meal (local food) S$20–35, coffee or soft drink (snack bar) S$2.

MRT (underground/subway). 50 cents–S$1.40 depending on distance.

Nightclubs/discotheques/cabarets. Obligatory first drink S$6–8.

Sightseeing. City Tour (3½ hours) S$19, East Coast Tour (3½ hours) S$16, Harbour Cruise (2½ hours) S$20, Malacca (full day) S$68. (Most tours are half price for children).

Taxis. Drop rate S$1.80 for first 1,500 metres, 10 cents for each subsequent 300 metres, surcharges for waiting time, luggage, etc.

Trains (one way, air-conditioned). Singapore–Kuala Lumpur S$28, Singapore–Butterworts (Penang) S$43.30.

Trishaws. S$16–20 for short ride in tourist area (after firm bargaining), S$35 for organized tour including Singapore Sling.

An A–Z Summary of Practical Information and Facts

> A star (*) following an entry indicates that relevant prices are to be found on page 107.

A   **AIRPORTS*.** Singapore's international airport at Changi, one of the largest in South-East Asia, can accommodate some 14 million passengers a year. In the ultra-modern complex are baggage trolleys and lockers, two full-service banks, currency exchange bureaux, a post office, telephone, telegram and telex services and duty-free shops (it even has a duty-free shop for arriving passengers who prefer not to carry their bargain whisky, cigarettes and perfume from the start of the flight). There's also a hotel and tour booking office, car hire desks, a clinic, nursery and "day rooms" for resting between flights. Ten restaurants and bars serve everything from drinks and snacks to Chinese, Japanese and Western specialities. Moving walkways shrink the distance from departure lounge to gate.

You'll have to take a taxi to get into town.

Leaving Singapore, all passengers must pay an airport departure tax (lower only for flights to Malaysia).

Airport flight information, tel.: 541 8888

C   **CAR HIRE.*** In addition to car-hire counters at the airport and agencies in the hotel district, the Singapore Yellow Pages list a number of local firms under "Motorcar Renting and Leasing" which may be somewhat cheaper. Self-drive and chauffeured cars, most of them air-conditioned, are available at hourly, daily and weekly rates. Some companies permit you to drop off your hired car at such Malaysian centres as Penang and Kuala Lumpur. (Surcharges apply where cars are taken out of Singapore.) A deposit has to be paid, though this is normally waived for holders of accepted credit cards. Apart from a valid driving licence, firms insist on a minimum age of either 21 or 23, and may refuse to rent a car to anyone over 60. Note that to drive into or hire your car within the Central Business District—CBD ("Restricted Zone")—between 7.30 and 10.15 a.m. or 4.30 and 7 p.m. from Monday to Saturday, you must buy a daily Area Licence (see DRIVING).

CIGARETTES, CIGARS, TOBACCO. Smoking is officially very unpopular in Singapore: under the government's campaign to discourage what it calls a "recognized health hazard", smoking is banned in such public places as lifts, buses, air-conditioned taxis, cinemas and theatres; the fine for violating this ban can be S$500 or more. However, the Republic's shops carry an extremely wide range of tobacco products. Note that prices are *not* duty-free except at the airport past Customs.

CLOTHING. Short-sleeved sportswear, with perhaps a light wrap for protection against arctic air-conditioning, is really all an average tourist needs in Singapore. No matter how monumental the showers in monsoon season, an umbrella is wiser than a raincoat in this tropical climate.

Dress is normally very casual; only a few places require a jacket and tie. However, suits and dresses will never be out of place in better restaurants and nightspots. Male business visitors will find shirt and tie, without jacket, customary attire.

COMMUNICATIONS

Post offices: Singapore has post offices in Tanglin Road, Collyer Quay opposite Clifford Pier, and Killiney Road just off Orchard Road, among others. The last is the only one open on Sundays and every other day of the year; all post offices close overnight.

Telexes are the domain of the Telecommunication Authority of Singapore (Telecoms), which also accepts **telegrams** at its locations separate from post offices.

Telephone: Within the Republic, calls are free on private and hotel room telephones, only 10 cents for three minutes on public phones—which goes a long way towards explaining why young Singaporeans spend so much time telephoning. Public phones carry clear instructions in English.

Singapore is now linked with most countries by international direct dialling; otherwise, the international phone exchange operates courteously and efficiently around the clock. To book a call in advance, dial 104.

International direct dialling (IDD) payphones which accept major credit cards are located at the airport and post offices. You'll also find "World Phones", coin-operated or using phone cards (sold in denominations of $10 to $50). And Home Country Direct Phonelink devices provide a line to an operator in selected countries, including the U.K., North America and Australia. From among the convenient possibilities of Telecoms service, you might choose to make your international call in luxurious surroundings at the air-conditioned Telephone House in Hill Street.

Singapore's telephone directories, including Yellow Pages, are in English and Chinese and new editions are issued annually.

The phone book warns: "Avoid using the telephone during thunderstorms."

COMPLAINTS. Singapore's authorities are diligent about promoting honesty, courtesy and other virtues visitors appreciate. You'll probably find little or nothing to complain about in this disciplined Republic, but incidents do, of course, occur. If it's something you can't sort out with the owner or manager of an establishment, report the problem to the Singapore Tourist Promotion Board (see TOURIST INFORMATION OFFICES). That includes any approach by a tout, which might also be reported to your hotel concierge. Taxi drivers who attempt to overcharge or short-change you should abandon that with alacrity if you take out a pen and make a note of their number plate. Otherwise, report their transgressions to:

Registry of Vehicles, Sin Ming Drive; tel.: 459 4222.

CONVERTER CHARTS. For fluid and distance measures, see page 112. Singapore uses the metric system.

Temperature

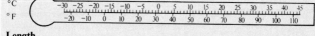

Length

Weight

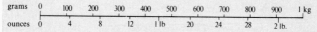

COURTESIES. One reason for the remarkable social harmony in Singapore is that other peoples' customs are automatically respected. Visitors should do the same. This means removing footwear before entering a mosque or Indian temple, for instance.

If you're the host at a meal for Singaporeans, before ordering be sure to check if anyone cannot eat certain dishes (Moslems, for example, do not eat pork). When dining off banana leaves at Indian restaurants, follow custom and use only your right hand.

If invited to a local home, it's polite to take along some fruit (oranges—for good luck—are appropriate for traditional Chinese families, but make sure they're in even numbers!). Entering most Singaporean homes, you'll want to do as others have and shed your shoes or sandals. And, when drinking anything offered by your host, leave a bit in the glass or cup as a sign of appreciation—to drink everything down to the last drop is thought of as greedy.

Business visitors should expect to hand out their calling cards at every conceivable encounter—and to receive one. The cards should be presented and received with both hands!

CRIME. Singapore has the lowest crime rate in all of South-East Asia, and by general world standards it's an exceptionally safe city. Violence is very rare and certainly shouldn't affect visitors. Pickpockets might be operating around People's Park in Chinatown and other crowded shopping complexes. Penalty for purse snatching is typically severe: 3 years in prison and 4 strokes of the rotan. Safety boxes and security guards in lobbies help keep hotel crime low. Uniformed and plainclothes police are particularly vigilant around the Orchard Road hotel area, though male visitors may be accosted here by the occasional persistent pimp.

DRIVING IN SINGAPORE (see also CAR HIRE). Visitors to the Republic can drive with their national licences or international driving permits. Cars may be imported for up to one year under a *carnet de passage*, which is not required for motorcycles.

Driving conditions: Regulations in this former British colony follow those in the United Kingdom: drive on the left, pass on the right, traffic already circling a roundabout (traffic circle) has precedence, yield to pedestrians at designated crossing spots. Within the city and in "accident-prone" areas, the speed limit is 50 kilometres per hour (31 m.p.h.), on the open road 70 (44 m.p.h.), 80 k.p.h. (50 m.p.h.) along expressways.

Singapore's roads are generally well paved and signposted. But they are crowded: the little Republic has about 300,000 motor vehicles (half

D of them cars and buses), and traffic jams can on occasion reach monumental proportions—particularly at peak periods on the Johore Strait causeway to Malaysia and in the Orchard Road hotel area. To reduce congestion in central Singapore for morning commuters, an area licence scheme has been introduced whereby a driver must pay a daily fee of several dollars to enter or drive within the Central Business District (CBD) between 7.30 and 10.15 a.m. and 4.30 and 7. p.m. from Monday to Saturday; you're exempted only if your car has four people or more in it. Booths just outside the zone sell the licences which must be displayed on the windscreen.

For much of the rest of the day, traffic is very heavy along Orchard Road. You'll notice some instances where local drivers are inconsiderate, and overtaking on the inside lane is a frequent abuse. Be prepared to think for other road users!

Parking: You must pay to park everywhere in metropolitan Singapore, although your hotel may give you a free sticker for its own premises. A unique coupon parking system (but confusing to the uninitiated) operates at most public car parks, including street-side parking. Parked cars must display the relevant parking ticket indicating date and time of arrival in their front windscreen. Parking coupons are sold at kiosks in booklets of ten. Charges differ, but are clearly signposted on orange/blue signs at regular intervals.

Drinking and driving: Your car insurance is not valid for an accident if, when tested, your blood is found to contain more than a small, designated amount of alcohol. Police are quick to pull over vehicles driven erratically, and penalties are heavy. Skulls and crossbones accompany frequent television spots warning: "Drink, Drive, Death".

Fuel and oil: Internationally known brands are available at Singapore's service stations. Fuel and oil are sold by the litre.

Fluid measures

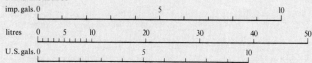

Distance

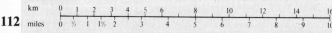

Breakdowns: Singapore has many garages. The larger car hire firms have stand-by mechanics or will provide a replacement vehicle should yours develop engine trouble.

Singapore's Automobile Association (AA) operates a 24-hour road service, telephone 748 9911.

DRUGS. An intensive educational and media campaign plus energetic police efforts and penalties—going as far as capital punishment—have succeeded in sharply reducing Singapore's narcotics problem. Drug smuggling and peddling inevitably occur; arrests are frequent and well publicized. The use of sniffer dogs at the airport has reportedly all but eliminated drug traffic there, and the animals have recently been put to work at the Johore causeway.

ELECTRIC CURRENT. Singapore's current is 220–240 volts, 50-cycle AC. If your hotel doesn't have an adaptor for your plug, shops will.

EMBASSIES, HIGH COMMISSIONS, CONSULATES. Few foreign missions are open on Saturdays, all close on Sundays. Many function for the public only on weekday mornings.

Australia: High Commission, 25 Napier Road; tel.: 737 9311.

Canada: High Commission, 80 Anson Road, hex 14-00, IBM Building; tel.: 225 6363.

Great Britain: High Commission, Tanglin Road; tel.: 473 9333.

India: High Commission, 31 Grange Road; tel.: 737 6809.

Ireland: Consulate, 541 Orchard Road, hex 08-02, Liat Towers; tel.: 732 3430.

New Zealand: High Commission, 13 Nassim Road; tel.: 235 9966.

Philippines: Embassy, 20 Nassim Road; tel.: 737 3977.

U.S.A.: Embassy, 30 Hill Street; tel.: 338 0251.

Denmark: Embassy, Thomson Road, hex 13-01, United Square; tel.: 250 3383.

Finland: Embassy, Newton Road, hex 21-02/03, United Square; tel.: 254 4042.

Norway: Embassy, 16 Raffles Quay, hex 44-01, Hong Leong Building; tel.: 220 7122.

Sweden: Embassy, 111 Somerset Road, hex 05-08, PUB Building, Devonshire Wing; tel.: 734 2771.

ENTRY FORMALITIES and CUSTOMS CONTROLS. Citizens of the British Commonwealth, Western Europe, North and South America need only a valid passport to enter Singapore for a tourist visit. Under usual circumstances, neither a cholera nor a yellow fever vaccination certificate is required. You will be given an immigration card to fill in on your plane before landing, the stub of which should be kept with your passport and surrendered on departure from the Republic.

Essentially a duty-free port, Singapore permits import and export without charge of practically all items of interest to tourists. Permits are required to bring in or take out such things as weapons, ammunition and more than reasonable personal effects of gold, platinum and precious stones. There is a strict ban against importing so-called "girlie" magazines, even the most popular "quality" journals sold widely all over the world. Video tapes may be impounded (except blanks).

The following chart shows what main duty-free items you may take into Singapore and, when returning home, into your own country.

Into:	Cigarettes		Cigars		Tobacco	Spirits		Wine
Singapore	200	or	50	or	250 g.	1 l.	and	1 l.
Australia	200	or	250 g.	or	250 g.	1 l.	or	1 l.
Canada	200	and	50	and	900 g.	1.1 l.	or	1.1 l.
Eire	200	or	50	or	250 g.	1 l.	and	2 l.
N.Zealand	200	or	50	or	½ lb.	1 qt.	and	1 qt.
S.Africa	400	and	50	and	250 g.	1 l.	and	1 l.
U.K.	200	or	50	or	250 g.	1 l.	and	2 l.
U.S.A.	200	and	100	and	*	1 l.	or	1 l.

* a reasonable quantity

Currency restrictions: There's no limit to the amount of Singapore and foreign currency or traveller's cheques you can bring into or take out of the Republic.

GUIDES. If you'd like a privately conducted tour, use only the guides trained and licensed by STPB (see TOURIST INFORMATION OFFICES) who wear special badges and carry documentation. Tours are a minimum of three hours at rates lower for English-speaking guides than for those speaking other languages. Group tours run by commercial agencies are normally escorted by STPB-licensed guides. Call the Singapore Tourist Guide Association at 338 3441 for advice. In any case, pick up the latest version of the *Singapore Official Guide* on arrival at the airport information counter.

HAIRDRESSERS'. In or near Singapore's tourist hotels you'll find a variety of barbers' and hairdressers', including a few who advertise links with noted foreign establishments.

Although more tolerant now than in the past, the Singapore government continues to frown on men with long hair. However, unless your locks are of Samsonian proportions, you have no problem with the authorities.

HITCH-HIKING. Don't bother: drivers will rarely pick anyone up, and anyway bus and taxi services are excellent and inexpensive.

HOTELS*. See also YOUTH HOSTELS. A recent construction boom has left Singapore with hotel rooms to spare. The resultant competition has reduced rates to well below advertised levels, so be sure to negotiate a discount—particularly if you're staying for more than three or four days. The quality of accommodation and service is high by international standards. Many establishments have swimming pools. The lower-priced hotels may not be fully air-conditioned. Most leading hotels, including some affiliated with large international chains, are in the Orchard Road area. Information on hotels is available at the arrival hall of Changi Airport.

JAY-WALKING. You could be fined as much as S$50 if caught crossing a road illegally. If you're within 50 yards of a pedestrian

J crossing such as a zebra or an overpass, use it or risk being ticketed. Signs showing a pedestrian with a line drawn through him mark the 50-yard limit on either side of a crossing. Beyond those limits, you're guided by common sense about the traffic, not by the law. The policeman who catches you could well be in plain clothes.

L **LANGUAGES.** You're excused if you're confused about Singapore's bewilderingly polyglot scene. The national language is Malay, fluently spoken by only about 15 per cent of the population though understood by most Singaporeans. The great Chinese majority (76 per cent) speaks one or more of the southern dialects—Hokkien, Teochew, Cantonese, Hainanese, Hakka, Foochow (listed in order of size of dialect group). Mandarin, the northern dialect, is being promoted by the government as Singapore's official language as it is in China and Taiwan.

The Republic's ethnic Indians speak mainly Telugu, Malayalam, Punjabi, Hindi and/or Bengali—not to mention their official Singaporean language, Tamil. If you're listening around the island, you'll also hear snatches of Urdu and Gujarati. There are others.

So to avoid complete communications chaos among themselves and with the huge tourist influx, most Singaporeans speak English. Therein lies a tale:

Singapore English is a delight. Spoken with a variety of Oriental lilts, it unquestionably sounds more musical than on either side of the Atlantic or "down under". Nostalgia enthusiasts will cherish all the old British and American clichés in everyday use here, even among schoolchildren.

Then there are such local oddities as "Is it?" This is the universal, if usually illogical, response showing mild interest or surprise. As in:

He: "You look beautiful tonight."   *She:* "Is it?"

or

"That bus doesn't go there…"   "Is it?"

And, of course, there's "la". This familiar expression is added to phrases or short sentences for emphasis, as in "Very hot-la" or "Come on-la" or "No-la".

Some typical Singapore expressions are reminiscent of the Caribbean: "Take 20 cents go" (to brush someone off), "Catch no ball" (don't understand), or "So late still don't come" (an airport favourite).

These and many others you'll hear from perfectly well-educated Singaporeans add to the exoticism for English-speaking visitors (if perhaps confusing others). Happy listening.

116

LAUNDRY and DRY-CLEANING. Hotels provide efficient but expensive service, normally charging an additional 50 per cent for "express" return of articles within a few hours. Singapore has several laundromats.

LITTER. Not by good will alone has Singapore become Asia's cleanest city. If you're caught tossing a piece of paper, cigarette end or any other refuse onto the ground, the fine ranges from S$50 for the first offence to S$250 or even S$500 for frequent offenders. Reminded by "Do Not Litter—S$500 Fine" signs all around town, you'll be prudent if you emulate all the Singaporeans you'll notice looking for refuse containers or putting whatever it is into their pockets.

LOST PROPERTY. If you've forgotten something in a bus or taxi, contact the Registry of Vehicles Department, locally called ROV (see COMPLAINTS), as chances are good it will turn up there. Otherwise, report your loss to the police. Hotels ceremonially and financially encourage their staffs to be honest about turning in guests' lost or forgotten items.

MAPS. For most tourists' needs, the Singapore maps available at hotels and the STPB are adequate, though they tend to lag behind developments in this city of rapid change. Which "tourist attractions" appear may depend on which commercial firm puts out the map. For detailed street plans or marine charts try a bookstore. If you intend to travel by bus, make sure you obtain an up-to-date bus guide as well.

The maps in this book are by Falk-Verlag, Hamburg.

MEDICAL CARE. Since Singapore has no free health service, you'll want to make certain your regular medical insurance will cover expenses should you fall ill here. Most hotels have doctors on call; all doctors are listed in the Yellow Pages under "Medical Practitioners". Dental surgeons are listed separately. To locate a specific doctor at any hour, dial 532 4865, where an island-wide beeper paging service used by most—but not all—doctors means you can make contact at all times. There's good ambulance service (dial 995, or the police, tel. 999) to government hospitals. You may later choose to transfer to one of the Republic's private hospitals. In general, facilities at Singapore's two dozen state or private hospitals are considered among the best in Asia. And thanks to such things as strict sanitary regulations and an actice anti-mosquito campaign, the island has practically no cases of the major tropical diseases.

M   Singapore's chemists' (drugstores) do not operate all-night service. After about 10 p.m. until 8 a.m., you'll be able to obtain medicine only at hospitals or through a doctor.

MEETING PEOPLE. Although Singapore is overwhelmingly young, the free and easy "singles culture" hasn't a toehold here yet. Visitors are often struck by how shy local people are, even those whose English is excellent. (This is truer of the Chinese than of the Malays or Indians.) But breaking the ice is easy—start a conversation in a friendly fashion and most Singaporeans will quickly respond.

There are no serious taboos about associating with foreigners—the Republic's racial mix is too rich for that. At hotel coffee houses or cinemas, in shopping centres or offices, on buses or ferries you'll have opportunities to initiate contact with Singaporeans.

Young ladies often go about in twos or threes, but that shouldn't discourage a lone male. Singapore men are rarely unreceptive to social approaches by foreign women, although they're heard to say they prefer their own petite or more feminine girls. You'll see all kinds of mixed couples.

MONEY MATTERS

Currency: The Singapore dollar (abbreviated \$, S\$ or SID) is divided into 100 cents, with coins of 1, 5, 10, 20 and 50 cents and S\$1. Banknotes in circulation are: S\$1, 5, 10, 20, 50, 100 and, more rarely, 500, 1,000 and 10,000. Brunei notes of the same denominations occasionally appear and are accepted interchangeably with Singapore money. Malaysian notes will not be. For currency restrictions, see under ENTRY FORMALITIES AND CUSTOMS CONTROLS.

Banking hours: 10 a.m. to 3 p.m., Monday to Friday, and 9.30 to 11.30 a.m. on Saturdays (for local banks and larger foreign banks only). However, several big local banks—usually at underground stations and major shopping centres—are open till 5 p.m. (7 p.m. in some cases) on Saturdays. At the airport bank you can exchange money and traveller's cheques around-the-clock.

Changing Money: Money is big business in Singapore: bank listings take 10 full Yellow Pages in the telephone directory, and there are even more money changers. The best rate can be had from licensed money changers (do not go to an unofficial one); it's usually a few cents better than at a bank. There are no real "deals" with Singapore's dollar, a very stable currency. But after checking the daily bank rate, shop around and bargain if you're exchanging a sizeable amount. Except in an emergency, avoid changing money at a hotel, where the rate is invariably poor.

Credit Cards and Traveller's Cheques: Major international credit and bank cards and traveller's cheques are widely accepted around Singapore. In most cases you'll need your passport. "Personal cheques not accepted" is a frequently posted sign here.

NEWSPAPERS and MAGAZINES. In addition to Singapore's English-language newspapers—*Straits Times, Business Times* and a racy afternoon tabloid *The New Paper*—you'll find some British and continental European dailies (on sale in the hotel district about two days after publication). The *International Herald Tribune,* edited in Paris and transmitted by satellite, is simultaneously published in Singapore. There are also four local Chinese papers, two in Tamil, one in Malay and one in Malayalam.

The *Singapore Tatler,* a monthly magazine, reports on the social and cultural scene, while various magazines for tourists, distributed free in the hotels, keep tabs on what's happening in town.

The vast array of local, regional and international magazines sold here does not include any of the well-known "girlie" glossies or anything else considered improper by the censors.

PHOTOGRAPHY. Not only does Singapore offer marvellous bargains in camera equipment and film, there are all kinds of colourful scenes you'll want to photograph. Normally local people don't mind being snapped, providing you ask permission. It's also best to ask before taking a photo inside any temple or mosque. At certain tourist attractions you'll be charged a nominal fee to use your camera.

Singapore's heat and humidity can damage your film and camera: keep them cool as much as possible. If you're shooting Kodachrome, save the film for processing at home, as the normal procedure here is to ship to Australia, which takes about a fortnight. If you are not fussy, numerous "instant" processing shops abound to develop your roll of film in a few hours. It costs more to develop within an hour. Prices are usually listed. Normal processing takes 1–2 days.

POLICE. Friendly and helpful to tourists, Singapore's police force is an efficient, respected part of society. Many of the police you see will seem young, which is in keeping with this youthful Republic. Those dressed in white control traffic. The Tanglin Police Station on Napier Road is nearest the hotel district.

Police emergency number: 999.

P **PUBLIC HOLIDAYS.** (See also Festivals, p. 87.) Singapore has 11 public holidays when much, if not all, commercial activity ceases and government offices close. If a holiday falls on a Sunday, it's celebrated the following day.

Fixed public holidays: January 1 (New Year's Day), May 1 (Labour Day), August 9 (National Day), December 25 (Christmas Day).

Movable holidays: Chinese New Year (two days), Good Friday, Vesak Day, Hari Raya Puasa, Deepavali, Hari Raya Haji.

R **RADIO and TV.** Singapore's AM radio service broadcasts daily from early morning until midnight in English, Chinese, Malay and Tamil, and there's also an FM stereo service often available in hotel rooms. Regional transmitting stations ensure good audibility of BBC World Service and Voice of America English-language shortwave programmes at various times during the day (early morning and evening are best). The BBC World Service is also relayed locally on FM for 12 hours daily. Some visitors may be interested to tune into Hanoi, Peking and Moscow English-language services for South-East Asia. German and French broadcasts are also heard clearly on shortwave.

Singapore has three TV channels which broadcast in the four languages. American adventure and comedy serials and ageing films are popular presentations. Three channels from two Malaysian TV stations, which have some programmes in English, are also received in Singapore.

RELIGIOUS SERVICES. Looking under "Temples", "Churches" and "Mosques" in the Yellow Pages will give you an idea of the tremendous variety and quantity of places of worship in Singapore. Practically every Christian denomination has at least one church here, and there are two synagogues. Ask your hotel reception for a listing of nearby churches and service times.

S **SIGHTSEEING HOURS**

Singapore:

Botanic Gardens: daily from dawn to 11 p.m.; admission free.

Crocodile Farm: daily from 8.30 a.m. to 5 p.m.

"Instant Asia" Cultural Show: daily including holidays at 11.30 a.m.

Japanese and Chinese Gardens: daily from 9.30 a.m. to 6 p.m.; nominal entry fee (combined admission available).

Jurong Bird Park: daily from 9 a.m. to 6 p.m.; small entry fee.

Mandai Orchid Garden: daily from 9 a.m. to 5.30 p.m.; a small admission fee is refundable against any purchase.

National Museum: daily except Mondays from 9 a.m. to 4.30 p.m.; admission fee charged.

Singapore Science Centre: daily except Monday from 10 a.m. to 6 p.m.; small entry fee.

Tiger Balm Gardens: daily from 10 a.m. to 6 p.m.; admission free.

Van Kleef Aquarium: daily from 9.30 a.m. to 9 p.m.; small entry fee.

Zoological Gardens: daily from 8.30 a.m. to 6 p.m.; small entry fee.

Penang:

Snake Temple: daily from 8.30 a.m. to 6 p.m.

Bali:

Denpasar Museum: mornings except Monday and holidays.

SIGHTSEEING TOURS* (typical examples):

City Tour: 3 to 3½ hours; *route:* Elizabeth Walk, Supreme Court, City Hall, Singapore River, Chinatown, Sri Mariamman Hindu Temple, Mount Faber, "Instant Asia" Cultural Show, Tiger Balm Gardens, Queenstown Housing Estate, Botanic Gardens National Museum.

City and East Coast Tour: 6 to 7 hours; *route:* combination of City Tour and East Coast Tour; lunch included.

East Coast Tour: 3 to 3½ hours; *route:* Merdeka Bridge, National Stadium, East Coast Park, Malay villages, fishing ponds, rubber and coconut plantations, Crocodile Farm, Temple of 1,000 Lights.

Flora and Fauna Tour: 3 to 5 hours; *route:* Mandai Orchid Gardens, Zoological Gardens (admission fee for cameras).

Harbour Cruises: 1-hour cruises at 10 a.m., 12.30 and 3 p.m., Monday to Saturday, except public holidays. *Sunset Harbour Cruise* (2 hours round Kusu and St. John's islands) at 7.15 p.m. daily. *Harbour and Island Cruise* (2½ hours with a 20-minute stop at Kusu Island) at 9.30 a.m. and 3.30 p.m., Monday to Saturday, except public holidays. Half-hour Singapore River cruises. *Harbour, Sentosa and Cable Car Tour* (3 hours) at 9.30 a.m. and 3.30 p.m., Monday to Saturday, except public holidays.

Junk Cruises: 2 and 2½-hour cruises on Chinese junk (around the harbour and southern islands) at 10.30 a.m., 3 p.m. and 4 p.m. daily. **121**

S *Jurong Tour:* 3 to 4 hours; *route:* Jurong Town, Jurong Bird Park, Chinese Garden (admission fee for cameras).

Dinner Cruises: 3 hours; harbour and islands with Singapore or Nonya buffet served on board; at 6 p.m. Wednesdays and Saturdays.

Night Tours: 2 to 6-hour sightseeing tours; sightseeing, cultural show and drink; sightseeing, cultural show and dinner; *route:* Elizabeth Walk, harbour, Chinatown, Mount Faber, Raffles Hotel (cultural show and dinner). Some include People's Park Shopping Complex, Sri Mariamman Hindu Temple, National Theatre, Van Kleef Aquarium, Satay Club.

Trishaw Tour: 1 hour and 3 hours; *route:* waterfront and through Chinatown.

T **TIME DIFFERENCES.** Singapore time year-round is GMT plus 8 hours. The following chart shows the time in January in some selected cities. In March/April, when British and U.S. clocks advance one hour, Singapore stays the same.

Los Angeles	New York	London(GMT)	**Singapore**	Tokyo	Sydney
2 a.m.	5 a.m.	10 a.m.	**6 p.m.**	7 p.m.	9 p.m.

TIPPING. In cases where a 10 per cent service charge (in addition to the 3 per cent government tax) is on your bill, leave nothing or just a few coins. Signs at the airport advise you not to tip porters, but you'll notice they have come to expect something if you're an obvious foreigner. For special service anywhere, a reasonable gratuity is in order.

Rough guidelines:

Bellboy, errand	S$1
Maid, per day	S$1
Hairdresser/Barber	S$1 (optional)
Porter, per bag	50¢
Tourist guide	5–10%
Waiter	10% if service charge not included

TOILETS. "Gentlemen" and "Ladies", which may otherwise be labelled with male and female symbols, are found in hotel lobbies, shopping centres, large stores, restaurants, cinemas and at most tourist attractions. They're well marked. Most charge a small fee.

A small fee is charged for the use of public toilets, which are regularly inspected by health officers. Fines (up to S$ 500) are imposed on users caught not flushing. However, first-time offenders, especially foreigners, may be let off with a warning.

TOURIST INFORMATION OFFICES

Australia: Singapore Tourist Promotion Board, 8th Floor, Goldfields House, 1 Alfred Street, Circular Quay, Sydney, N.S.W. 2000; tel.: 241-3771/2. Cable: TOURISPROM SYDNEY.

Suite 3, 336 Churchill Avenue, Subiaco, W.A. 6008; tel.: 381-1855.

Great Britain: Singapore Tourist Promotion Board, Carrington House, 126–130 Regent Street, London WIR 5FE; tel.: 437-0033. Cable: TOURISPROM LONDON-W1.

New Zealand: c/o Rodney Walshe Ltd, 2nd Floor, Dingwell Building, 87 Queen Street, P.O. Box 279, Auckland 1; tel.: (9) 793–708.

U.S.A.: Singapore Tourist Promotion Board, Suite 1008, 342 Madison Avenue, New York, NY 10017; tel.: 687-0385. Cable: TOURISPROM NEW YORK.

251 Post Street, San Francisco, CA 94108; tel.: (415) 391-8476. Cable: TOURISPROM SAN FRANCISCO.

Singapore: Singapore Tourist Promotion Board, Raffles City Tower 36–04, 250 North Bridge Road, Singapore 0617; tel.: 339 6622.

Tourist Information Centre, Raffles City Shopping Centre, hex 01-19; tel.: 330 0431 or 330 0432.

Hours: 8 a.m. to 5 p.m., Monday–Friday, till 1 p.m. on Saturdays.

TRANSPORT

Buses:* Frequent, convenient and very cheap, Singapore's public buses are a fine way to go almost everywhere on the island. They operate with open windows instead of air-conditioning between 6 a.m. and 11.30 p.m. Avoid rush hours. An inexpensive booklet listing all bus routes is on sale, but normally it's even simpler to ask friendly Singaporeans at

T any bus stop. Many services operate one-way down Orchard Road past major hotels, and back along the parallel Somerset Road–Orchard Boulevard route.

Within the Central Business District (CBD), you can get around easily by using the Shuttle Bus Services CBD1 and CBD2. Both buses take passengers to the major hotels in Orchard Road, to shopping centres and some places of interest, including Singapore Handicraft Centre, Rasa Singapura Food Centre and other tourist attractions. CBD1 also stops at the Botanic Gardens.

These shuttle services operate at 10-minute intervals for a flat fare per passenger per trip. Each bus is operated by a driver only, so remember to have the exact fare with you. Explorer tickets are available for one or three days of unlimited travel on both city and trans-island routes. Services run between 9.10 a.m. and 5 p.m. on weekdays (9.10 a.m.– 12.30 p.m. and 3.30 p.m.–8 p.m. on Saturdays), but do not oper- ate on Sundays or public holidays. For information, call the Singa- pore Bus Service, tel.: 287 2727.

Long-distance coaches, some air-conditioned, operate regularly to points within Malaysia. The trip to Penang/Butterworth, with a stop at Malacca (after about 4 hours), lasts 14 hours, while the Kuala Lumpur express takes 9 hours.

Underground/Subway: The Mass Rapid Transit System (MRT) pro- vides a fast and convenient means of transport between the central shopping district and the CBD, as well as to most of the major satel- lite towns or housing estates, where the majority of the population live in government-built flats.

Taxis:* Singapore's taxis are in good condition—none can be more than seven years old by law. Cars with the "taxi" roof sign made of blue glass are air-conditioned. Fares (always metered) are reasonable. Note that between midnight and 6 a.m. there's a 50 per cent overnight surcharge over and above the meter reading. Drivers add a surcharge to fares when entering the Central Business District between 7.30 and 10.15 a.m. and when boarding a taxi in the CBD between 4 and 7 p.m. Avoid any taxi whose driver claims his meter isn't working.

Taxis are usually plentiful in the CBD and near most hotels, except when it rains. They're much scarcer out in the countryside. Book well ahead if you'll need a radio cab. In the Orchard Road area you can flag down taxis, but on some busy central streets you'll have to queue at formal taxi ranks. When business is slack, don't be surprised when taxi drivers hoot as they cruise by—it's just to let people know they're free.

Passengers (or drivers) caught smoking in air-conditioned taxis can be fined up to S$1,000 and even imprisoned for 3 months.

Singaporeans don't tip taxi drivers.

Trains: Daily services from Singapore run to such major Malaysian points as Kuala Lumpur and Butterworth (for Penang). There's less frequent service between Butterworth and Bangkok, Thailand. Fastest trains from Singapore reach Kuala Lumpur in about 7 hours, Butterworth in 13. Fares, which are reasonable, are higher for air-conditioned coaches.

Trishaws: Singapore still has about 1,000 of these bicycle-with-sidecar conveyances, which years ago replaced the human-drawn rickshaw in much of Asia. But they are declining in this city of good, inexpensive buses and taxis. Though housewives still use them for marketing trips, nowadays it's primarily tourists who keep trishawmen pedalling. You'll see some posted day and night near major hotels. Like Venice's gondoliers, trishaw drivers fighting to survive often ask exorbitant fares of tourists. You should bargain, determinedly, before setting off in a trishaw. They're useful only for short trips. Through your hotel or travel agencies, you can book group trishaw tours of Chinatown in the evening.

A handful of craftsmen are still making trishaws in Singapore, not only for local use, but also for export to collectors of nostalgia—notably in the U.S. and Britain.

WATER. Singapore's tap water is perfectly safe to drink, and everyone does. There is locally bottled mineral water, little used, and well-known European mineral waters are readily available from big supermarkets.

YOUTH HOSTELS. The YMCA and YWCA branches in Singapore have a total of less than 300 beds. Room rates are somewhat lower than at most hotels. Both accept married couples. Some rooms are air-conditioned and have private baths.

Index

An asterisk (*) next to a page number indicates a map reference. For index to Practical Information, see inside front cover.

INDEX

126

INDEX

128